TWO PLAYS

At My Heart's Core
&
Overlaid

Plays by Robertson Davies

Full length:
— *The King Who Could Not Dream*, written 1944, unproduced, unpublished.
— *King Phoenix*, written 1947, first production 1950. Toronto: New Press (in *Hunting Stuart and Other Plays*, edited by Brian Parker), 1972.
— *Benoni*, written 1945, produced by the Crest Theatre, Toronto, as *A Jig for the Gypsy*, 1954. Toronto: Clarke, Irwin, 1954.
— *Fortune, My Foe*, first production 1948. Toronto: Clarke, Irwin, 1949.
— *At My Heart's Core*, first production for Peterborough's centenary 1950. Toronto: Clarke, Irwin, 1950.
— *Hunting Stuart*, first production 1955. Toronto: New Press (*Hunting Stuart and Other Plays*, edited by Brian Parker), 1972.
— *General Confession*, never produced. Toronto: New Press (in *Hunting Stuart and Other Plays*, edited by Brian Parker), 1972.
— *Love and Libel*, adaptation of novel *Leaven of Malice*, Broadway production 1960. *Canadian Drama* 7, no. 2 (1981): 117-190, *Leaven of Malice: A Theatrical Extravaganza*.
— *Question Time*, first production at St. Lawrence Centre, Toronto, 1975. Toronto: Macmillan, 1975.
— *Pontiac and the Green Man*, performed at University of Toronto's sesquicentennial in 1975, unpublished.

One act:
— *Hope Deferred*, first produced 1948. Toronto: Clarke, Irwin (in *Eros at Breakfast and Other Plays*), 1949.
— *Overlaid*, first produced by the Ottawa Drama League 1947. Toronto: Samuel French, 1948.
— *Eros at Breakfast*, first production 1948. Toronto: Clarke, Irwin (*Eros at Breakfast and Other Plays*), 1949.
— *The Voice of the People*, written 1949, Davies directed first production in 1950. Toronto: Clarke, Irwin (in *Eros at Breakfast and Other Plays*), 1949.
— *At the Gates of the Righteous*, first produced 1948. Toronto: Clarke, Irwin (in *Eros at Breakfast and Other Plays*), 1949.

Masques:
— *A Masque of Aesop*, performed 1952 at Upper Canada College. Toronto: Clarke, Irwin, 1952, 1955.
— *A Masque of Mr. Punch*, performed 1963 at Upper Canada College. Toronto: Oxford University Press, 1963.

Television Drama:
— *Brothers in the Black Art*, broadcast by CBC 1974. Vancouver: Alcuin Society, 1981.

ROBERTSON DAVIES

TWO PLAYS

At My Heart's Core
&
Overlaid

 Simon & Pierre

We would like to express our gratitude to the Canada Council and the Ontario Arts Council for their support.

Marian M. Wilson, Publisher

1 2 3 4 5 · 5 4 3 2 1

Canadian Cataloguing in Publication Data

Davies, Robertson, 1913—
    At my heart's core ; and, Overlaid

ISBN 0-88924-225-9

I. Title. II. Title: Overlaid

PS8507.A67A8 1991   C812'.54   C91-094046-0
PR9199.D38A8 1991

Cover design: C.P. Wilson Graphic Communication
General Editor: Marian M. Wilson
Editors: Peter Goodchild, Jean Paton
Printer: Marc Veilleux Inc.

Printed in Canada

Contents

Introduction
by Robertson Davies

The two plays offered in this book have been performed many times in Canada, and I have seen several of these productions. The ones I liked best were those which recognized that *Overlaid* and *At My Heart's Core* are in no way realistic, but are theatrical in their nature and are best when performed with full theatricality.

What do I mean? Many theatre people are committed to what they call Realism, and their aim is to persuade the audience that it is looking at something that might occur in precisely the same way in daily life. Plays presented in this manner often have long passages in which real objects are employed to further the illusion of reality. Taken to its highest pitch this sort of theatre finds its pinnacle in a production by David Belasco (1859-1931) who astonished New York audiences in 1912 by representing an exact replica of a Child's Restaurant on stage, complete with real food! But the outward trappings of life are not the innermost secrets of life, and these are, in my opinion, best presented in a heightened form of theatre in which the dialogue, acting and setting are somewhat larger than life. Thus poetry of speech, histrionic accomplishment and fine designs can combine to speak to the audience of the deepest truths of life as it is in its most intense moments. This is painting, as opposed to photography.

Consider the short play *Overlaid*. To present it realistically misses its point entirely, for it is a protest about what people of imprisoned mind think of as "real." To Ethel reality is the outward appearance of respectability, to be careful never to give the neighbours anything to criticize, to aim toward the day when the whole family will be under total control, incapable of any wrong or absurd action, under a tombstone of uncompromising solidity and obvious expense. Contrasted with her is Pop, who yearns for a larger life than his farm has ever brought him, and who catches a whiff of it in the Saturday afternoon broadcasts from the Metropolitan Opera in New York. These two embody the opposed attitudes that Bernard Berenson called "life-diminishing" and "life-enhancing." If I had wanted to be fancy, I might have written a play in verse which was an argument between Eros, the spirit of life and love, and Thanatos, the spirit of Death. But that would not have been as much fun as setting the argument in a Canadian farmhouse kitchen, and embodying Life and Death in an eccentric old man who is determined to get everything out of his life that it can be made to yield, and his daughter, who is his superior in education, but not as brave a spirit, whose strongest desire is for the safety and respectability of the graveyard.

The best production of *Overlaid* that I have seen showed the farmhouse kitchen, tiny and very much distorted, against a wide panorama of the Canadian winter landscape, bleak and uncompromising. That was certainly not Realism, but it was a thrilling aspect of Theatricality, and it did much to assist the actors. Nobody in real life speaks like Pop; he is a vaudeville farmer.

But for that reason he is all farmers everywhere. And Ethel is like all life-haters everywhere. The play must be read as an abstraction from life and not as an attempt to depict life realistically. It is meant to make you laugh, but it will not be a foolish laugh.

This applies also to *At My Heart's Core*, a more elaborate treatment of the same theme, which is the cost in pain and bitterness of intellectual starvation.

Very often, when we are offered our Pioneer ancestors by playwrights or novelists, we are shown very humble people who have left Europe because of painful necessity, and whose enemies are want and starvation. There were others, and their troubles were different. They were educated people, usually with some money of their own, who came to Canada in search of adventure in a new land, or else in the hope of rising above whatever the old land seemed to offer them. The Stewarts are of the first group; Irish people of distinguished family and education, they wanted the excitement of a new life. That is to say, Thomas Stewart did so, but he did not give much consideration to his wife; indeed, he forbade her to bring her piano to Canada because he said that she might play Irish songs on it, and feel homesick. If he thought homesickness needed a piano to evoke it, he must have been a very simple man. The Moodies and the Traills came because they had little money and Canada seemed to offer chances that were more encouraging to two retired army officers than life in England. This was an illusion, for neither Moodie nor Traill was a man of much ability, and the height of their ambition was a safe government job, as the play makes clear.

It was the women who suffered. If there was any adventure, it was probably the men who enjoyed it. The women had to work as they had never worked before, and if their minds were not to rust and all the accomplishments that entitled them to think of themselves as ladies were not to wither away, they had to struggle, and often their pain must have been grievous. This is the theme of the play. At the heart's core there lingers the image of the dear native land

and the position that they had held in it. Mrs. Moodie and Mrs. Traill could not forget Reydon Hall, where they were raised, nor could Mrs. Stewart forget that she had once been a belle of the vice-regal court in Dublin, with distinguished suitors. If they had not chosen the husbands they did, might Mrs. Moodie and Mrs. Traill have found distinction in the literary and scientific worlds of London? Might Mrs. Stewart have been Lady Rossmore, with a husband who would not have denied her the piano or the luxuries of a refined life? This is what lies in the heart's core: the yearning for What Might Have Been.

These are not trivial discontents. They have to be faced and conquered if they are not to destroy the life that has been chosen.

The ladies are tempted, by the insidious Mr. Cantwell, who may perhaps be the Devil, for, as Hamlet assures us, the Devil may assume a pleasing shape. Indeed, the ladies are seduced. That word is often used as if it meant sexually possessed, and nothing more, but there are worse kinds of seduction than that. Cantwell does not tempt them into a brief infidelity to their marriage vows; he tempts them to be discontented with the choice they have made and the life it has brought them, and such a temptation could ruin their lives, poison their marriages, and turn them into bitter, wretched people forever. This is a terrible temptation, and Mrs. Moodie and Mrs. Traill do not fully escape it. Only Mrs. Stewart escapes, because of her real and deep love for her husband, who is a good man if not a particularly brilliant one.

Contrasted with the ladies and their husbands and their seducer are the Irish characters. Because this is an avowedly theatrical play they are funny and highly coloured, but they are not simple hooligans. Honour is of the stuff from which new countries are made; she is courageous, strong and undefeatable. Phelim is quite another thing. As he makes clear to Mrs. Moodie, he is descended from the great Irish line of bards and storytellers; his heritage is mythical and indestructible. Compared with the popular stories she writes for magazines, his heritage is glorious and hers is simply commercial and popular. Like many true artists he is a disreputable creature, but there are depths of nobility in him which shame Mrs. Moodie's genteel pretensions. Like Pop in *Overlaid*, Phelim is too big for the life in which he finds himself, and like Pop any escape he finds must be in tall talk and dreams.

All the talk in *At My Heart's Core* is tall talk, and it is the tall talk of 1837 when the accounts we have of conversations among Byron's friends, or the speeches politicians made to the public, tell us of a world where talk was of a copiousness and literary distinction that our age of radio and TV has wholly lost. Nowadays such talk is in the highest degree unrealistic, and good performances of the play have convinced me that I was right to make it what it is, for it convinces the hearer that these are truly people of 1837, and gives pleasure by its apparent artificiality and extravagance. A play is, after all, a work of art, or should be one, and artificiality and extravagance are accompaniments of art in many of its most pleasing forms.

Sometimes critics have rebuked me for making the theme of Canada's intellectual poverty the theme of several of my plays. But if I may speak in my own defence, critics normally live in big cities and mix with sophisticated people, whereas I have lived in places that were small and culturally under-nourished, and I know what that does to the people who live in such circumstances and have nothing upon which to hone the mind. The things of the spirit are fully as necessary as the things of the flesh, and where they do not exist a serious disease appears which I have called Cultural Rickets. And of course it must be remembered that these plays were written many years ago, and that things in Canada are changing, and intellectual isolation is not as severe as once it was. But I will not be moved from my conviction that what I have shown in my plays are certain aspects of truth, and the task of the playgoer, and the reader, is to find the truth wrapped in the theatricality.

Robertson Davies

Our Changing Speech
by Herbert Whittaker

We all know that speech patterns and vocabularies change with the times. Classic novels, the ones that survive their own era to enlighten and instruct succeeding generations, tell us how people spoke before our time. The drama gives us the most wonderful opportunity to hear how they sounded. Often they sound more exciting to our ears than our own everyday speech, when a fine writer provides the dialogue.

To convince us that his play is true to the historic past he is writing about, a modern dramatist must find a language different from the one he would use writing about today. In *At My Heart's Core*, Robertson Davies conjures up the past of Canadian life by giving his characters different rhythms, speech structure and vocabulary. Since his three principal characters were actually pioneer writers, he has their help in establishing this convincingly. As the players assume the language of these women, and the men in their lives, they will find it easy to assume their personae. Speaking the language common to the year 1837, they help Davies convince us of the truth of his argument, which is that artists have to struggle to survive in our own time to give us our own literature.

Davies lets us know through this play that the struggle exists today as it did when the country was in its more formative state, and he does so obliquely, seeming to aim his direct accusation at past conditions. Here the conventions of past speech are of great aid.

For centuries audiences have been adjusting willingly to a language which differed from their daily one. We recognize that if Shakespeare were to be translated into our own vocabulary, we would be reducing one of the world's treasures, a great dramatist-poet's creation for audiences of all generations.

We don't protest, then, when Davies has Pop, a character in *Overlaid*, say "she worked like a nigger on this farm," because he is bound by both the language and the prejudices of his day. Similarly, in *At My Heart's Core*, when Sally is referred to as "a heathen savage," we must respect Davies' accuracy of observation. He can trace the "savage" of the time through to the use of "Indian," and on to the current term "native people." The old labels survive in various ways. The leading black company in United States' theatre stills calls itself "The Negro Ensemble" to this day. And films about pioneer life in North America echo "The Indians are coming!" without audiences expecting an invasion of people from India.

If we are prepared to make the necessary concessions in speech, we are surely bound to make them in manners of speaking, by characters addressing people in different levels of society from their own, no matter how we deplore the class system this represents. We may defy the class system in literature altogether, but not be willing to sacrifice our favourite literary kings, queens and knights. So when the Moodies and the Traills speak down to Phelim and Honour we know they speak for their period, not ours.

Davies has observed this distinction and he realizes that if these pioneers spoke in that mannered fashion, the people they employed were likely to speak quite differently. Playwrights are always on the alert to tip off their audiences about their characters' backgrounds by emphasizing their dialect. George Bernard Shaw used this to great advantage in *Pygmalion*, which became a musical play called *My Fair Lady*, and let millions of people know that they are likely to be judged by their speech, but that they can do something about it if they want to.

H Whittaker

Herbert Whittaker is an influential voice in Canadian theatre, reviewer for the Montreal Gazette *and later the Toronto* Globe and Mail *from 1935 to 1975. He is also noted for his stage designs for the Montreal Repertory Theatre, Everyman Players, Hart House Theatre and Canadian Players. In 1976, Herbert Whittaker received the Order of Canada for his writing and his work on behalf of Canadian theatre organizations.*

At My Heart's Core

At My Heart's Core

Characters:

Mrs. Frances Stewart

Sally

Mrs. Catherine Parr Traill

Mrs. Susanna Moodie

Honour Brady

Phelim Brady

Mr. Edmund Cantwell

The Hon. Thomas Stewart, M.L.C., J.P.

The action takes place at Auburn, the home of the Stewarts in Douro settlement, on a December day in 1837.

First Production: The play was written for the centennial celebration of Peterborough, Ontario, Canada. Original cast for the first production by the Peterborough Summer Theatre on August 28, 1950, under the management of Michael Sadlier:

Mrs. Frances Stewart	Brenda Davies
Sally	Marjorie Root
Mrs. Catherine Parr Traill	Kate Reid
Mrs. Susanna Moodie	Clarine Jackman
Honour Brady	Pat Atkinson
Phelim Brady	Frank Perry
Mr. Edmund Cantwell	John Primm
The Hon. Thomas Stewart, M.L.C., J.P.	Donald Glen

Act One

(The scene is Auburn, the homestead of the **Honourable Thomas Alexander Stewart**, *a Member of the Legislative Council, in the district of Douro, in Upper Canada. The time is early in December, 1837.*

As we look at the stage most of it is filled by the house itself, which, standing at the audience's right, is open to us, like a doll's house. The room that we see is the best chamber; because this is the dwelling of settlers of some means and taste it is an attractive place. The logs which form the walls have been trimmed down to a flat, glowing wooden surface; the furniture is good, though plain, and is of mahogany and walnut; there are bookshelves filled with books, bound chiefly in leather, some maps, and two or three good engravings. In the left-hand wall, as we look from the audience, is a big fireplace with a wooden mantel, and over it hang guns and a few Indian trophies. On the mantel are some fossils, and on the walls are the skins of a few small animals, for **Mrs. Stewart** *is a naturalist of uncommon ability. Also in the left-hand wall is a window and the door to the outside. A door to kitchen quarters is on the right-hand side at the back. On the right-hand wall is a bunk bed, with curtains to shut in the sleepers; there is also a curtain which can be drawn parallel with the fireplace wall to cut this room in two, so that the occupant of the bunk may have space to dress in privacy.*

On the left we are able to see the dooryard and a part of the forest which surrounds the house, so that we can see people approach, as others are busy inside. The trees are bare, but no snow has fallen.

The curtain rises on a bright December morning. Inside the house there are some signs of disorder; a basin stands on the table and there are one or two towels on the floor; a large kettle sits on the hearth. The door at the back opens and **Mrs. Stewart** *and* **Sally** *enter, carrying between them a large pioneer cradle, which they place near the bed.*

Mrs. Frances Stewart *is a woman of unusually pleasing and youthful appearance, plainly dressed. When she speaks it is apparent that she is Irish and also a lady "brought up," as her friend Maria Edgeworth said, "in all the refinements of high cultivation." In other words, a real lady and not a spurious one. If possible, let her have a beautiful voice.*

Sally *is an Indian of indeterminate age, of pillowy figure. Her customary expression is a broad smile, and from time to time she giggles for no apparent reason. She wears a loose gown and moccasins, and has a few odds and ends of ill-chosen adornment.)*

Mrs. Stewart: Sally, clear away, will you.

(She goes to the bunk and tenderly lifts from it an infant, wrapped in a blanket.)

You've chosen a very strange time to settle in Douro, young person. And a girl, too! Don't you know we have too many girls in Douro already? What use are girls, young person, will you tell me? Don't you know that we need men, to fight the rebels? Don't you know that we need men to defend us from the outrageous and bloodthirsty Indians, like Sally?

*(**Sally** giggles hugely.)*

I'm really astonished at your impertinence, young person. Do you intend to take up an extensive piece of land? Pray oblige me by letting me inspect your settler's ticket.

(She solemnly inspects a tiny hand).

Ah, as I thought; no ticket. Now what do you suppose the Honourable Thomas Alexander Stewart, M.L.C., J.P., will say to a very young settler with no ticket?

Sally: Master, he laugh. He all time laugh. *(She laughs, herself.)*

Mrs. Stewart: Oh Sally, I wish he were here to laugh at this minute.

Sally: Master, he fine. He all time fine. Missus no fret.

Mrs. Stewart: I am not fretting, Sally. I positively deny that I am fretting. Still, a rebellion is no laughing matter.

*(But **Sally** laughs until she shakes all over.)*

Except to you, of course. Everything is a laughing matter to you. How your people acquired their reputation for impassiveness I shall never understand. Now, young person, into the cradle with you. And do not presume to stir until I have had my breakfast.

Sally: What you want?

Mrs. Stewart: Bring me the loaf and I shall make toast. And tea — the ordinary tea.

(Sally goes to the kitchen. Mrs. Stewart moves to the bed and gives a nurse's look at its occupant. Then she looks into the cradle, and tucks the infant a little more closely. Sally returns with a settler's loaf — cottage loaf — from which she cuts a slice, and spearing it on a toasting fork, sits down to prepare her mistress' breakfast. Mrs. Stewart sits in a chair, and seems disposed to sleep. It is at this point that Mrs. Moodie and Mrs. Traill appear through the woods, walking briskly. Though Mrs. Moodie is a year younger than her sister, she is the dominant one, and there is a ladylike hint of the drill-sergeant in her demeanour. Mrs. Traill is a gentle and abstracted person, whose characteristic expression is a charming but rather vague smile. They both wear large shawls and poke bonnets, and their dress is for use rather than style.)

Mrs. Traill: Frances has not yet been abroad, I perceive.

Mrs. Moodie: Sensible woman, to take her sleep when she can.

Mrs. Traill: Perhaps she has had good news.

Mrs. Moodie: We shall soon know.

(Mrs. Moodie knocks, and Mrs. Stewart starts in her chair; she quickly gains possession of herself, and draws the curtain which shuts off the bedroom part of the chamber. Then she admits them.)

Mrs. Stewart: Oh my dears, how very early you are abroad. Have you had some news?

Mrs. Moodie: That is what we have come to ask you.

Mrs. Stewart: No, nothing whatever.

Mrs. Moodie: Then it was only rumour after all.

Mrs. Stewart: Even a new rumour might be better than nothing. What have you heard?

Mrs. Traill: Very early this morning it came to our ears that a man in a red coat was seen at your door late last night. We thought that it might have been a messenger.

Mrs. Stewart: What a curious story.

Mrs. Traill: Then you have had no news?

Mrs. Stewart: No, none at all.

Mrs. Moodie: A red coat would be very conspicuous in the forest. A strange thing to make a mistake about.

Mrs. Stewart: At this time people have red coats on the brain.

Mrs. Moodie: The sight of a red coat would not trouble anyone whose loyalty was above question.

Mrs. Traill: Then we have had our walk for nothing.

Mrs. Stewart: Oh, please don't say that. You will have something to eat, won't you? You have not lost your journey when it gives me so much joy to see you. Pray sit down. You will take off your bonnets, will you not?

Mrs. Moodie: If I take off my bonnet, Frances, I warn you that I shall stay a long time.

Mrs. Stewart: Nothing could please me better.

(**Sally** *takes both bonnets and* **Mrs. Moodie**'s *shawl to the kitchen quarters. They both wear caps under their bonnets.*)

Mrs. Traill: But you have much to do. Are the children awake?

Mrs. Stewart: I sent them to Peterborough, to the Reverend Mr. Taylor two days ago. He is so very kind, and I thought that if I had to make a sudden journey, or the house were to be upset for any reason, it would be better not to distress them.

Mrs. Traill: I think that Peterborough must be full of settlers' children. Susanna and I sent ours there yesterday.

Mrs. Stewart: We really cannot keep them in the forest. Not that there is likely to be any danger, of course, but if there should be, they are much better off where there are men to defend them.

Mrs. Moodie: I have no very great opinion of the Peterborough militia. The best have already gone to York to fight the rebels there, and many of those who remain are Methodists.

Mrs. Stewart: But Susanna, I know several of them and they are most respectable persons.

Mrs. Moodie: Methodists are all very well, but they have a strong leaning toward rebellion.

Mrs. Stewart: Yes, it is most vexing of them, but it cannot be helped now. Do sit down. See, Sally has made quite a lot of toast, and we can begin.

Mrs. Moodie: Breakfast will be very welcome. We have walked quite eight miles.

Mrs. Traill: Oh, sister, we used to walk much greater distances in England and think nothing of it.

Mrs. Moodie: Very rarely before breakfast. I will make no secret of it; I am uncommonly sharp-set.

Mrs. Stewart: How fortunate. I have excellent grape jelly.

Mrs. Moodie: I dote upon grape jelly.

Mrs. Stewart: And we shall have real tea, for a treat.

Mrs. Moodie: None of your boilings of hemlock bark. How I detest that abominable apology for tea. I have almost taken to drinking whisky to avoid it.

Mrs. Traill: Susanna dear, you would make a stranger think that you were quite greedy.

Mrs. Stewart: As we are all females it is not necessary for Susanna to conceal the fact that she has an appetite.

Mrs. Moodie: I always have an appetite; I always have had one. Even when I was a romantic girl, and most in love, I never ceased to have an appetite. And now that I do a man's work, I believe I eat as much as a man.

Mrs. Stewart: I feel certain that it is the exercise of your intellectual powers which makes you so hungry, my dear. Thomas says that two hours of work over his books make him hungrier than a day pulling stumps. Have some toast.

(During this scene she is busy measuring tea from a caddy and infusing it, in making toast at the fire, and in attending to the wants of the others. **Sally** *goes to the kitchen.)*

Mrs. Traill: I do not think it quite right to say that you work like a man, Susanna. We all do a great many things, of course, that we would not do at home, but we must not lose our sense of proportion.

Mrs. Moodie: Let me say, then, that I work like an English farmer. That is how the women work in Upper Canada. As for the men — they work as horses might be expected to work in England. Does that restore the proportion?

Mrs. Stewart: Certainly one finds oneself doing things that would have been quite out of one's scope at home. You know, when I was a girl in Ireland, I used to turn quite faint at the sight of blood. Here I have bathed and bandaged I cannot guess how many wounds, not one of them caused by a quarrel, I am happy to say.

Mrs. Traill: And I hope it may continue so, my dear. But if the rebellion should not be so easily put down as we hope, some of us may be wanted as nurses.

Mrs. Stewart: Oh, we must trust that it will be a very short disturbance.

Mrs. Moodie: I am not hopeful of it. Those Methodists are uncommonly tenacious of a mistaken opinion.

Mrs. Stewart: My dear Susanna, you seem determined that it is all the fault of the Methodists.

Mrs. Moodie: And I am right. When you say Methodist, you say Radical. They all think that the world can be improved by rebellion against authority. It can't.

Mrs. Stewart: But Mackenzie leads the rebellion, and he is not a Methodist, I believe.

Mrs. Moodie: Mackenzie, I am perfectly convinced, is an atheist. But he knows how to get the Methodists to fight for him. They are opposed to authority and so is he.

Mrs. Traill: You are familiar with Susanna's "Oath," Frances, are you not?

Mrs. Stewart: No, but I have heard it spoken of. Would you be good enough to tell me about it, my dear?

Mrs. Moodie: Nothing would give me greater pleasure. It is merely a simple, rough thing that I threw off at white heat and dispatched at once to Montreal and to Toronto and to all the nearby papers. You must not expect any of the grace which critics have so kindly ascribed to my other things. It is called "The Oath of the Canadian Volunteers."

(She rises, brushes crumbs from her bosom, takes a commanding position on the hearth and declaims, not without effect.)

> Huzza for England! May she claim
> Our fond devotion ever;
> And by the glory of her name
> Our brave forefathers' honest fame
> We swear — no foe shall sever
> Her children from the parent's side;
> Though parted by the wave,
> In weal or woe, whate'er betide,
> We swear to die, or save
> Her honour from the rebel band
> Whose crimes pollute our injured land!

Mrs. Stewart: Oh how very stirring, my dear. Nothing about the Methodists yet?

Mrs. Traill: The Methodists do not come into the poem, Frances.

Mrs. Moodie: I do not consider Methodists, even in a time of crisis, to be the stuff of which poetry is made. Was your query intended to be ironical, Frances?

Mrs. Stewart: I am sorry. I should not have quizzed you, Susanna.

Mrs. Moodie: I shall not continue unless you wish it.

Mrs. Stewart: Oh, pray continue. Let us have it all.

Mrs. Moodie:
>Then courage, loyal volunteers!
>God will defend the right;
>That thought will banish slavish fears,
>That blessed consciousness still cheers
>The soldier in the fight.
>The stars for us will never burn,
>The stripes may frighten slaves,
>The Briton's eye will proudly turn
>Where Britain's standard waves.
>Beneath its folds, if Heaven requires
>We'll die, as died of old our sires!

Mrs. Stewart: Oh my dear, it is beautiful of course, but I wish that gloomy talk of dying didn't come in at the end of it.

Mrs. Moodie: That is merely poetic licence, my dear. If there is any dying to be done, it will be done by the rebels. Our husbands are, after all, professional soldiers, and officers. Where the danger is greatest, there they will be found, but not needlessly exposed.

Mrs. Traill: Surely you are not concerned for Mr. Stewart? He is a civilian; how could he be in danger?

Mrs. Stewart: I have not had your experience in these matters. You are soldiers' wives; you have learned not to be foolishly concerned. It would be such a very great misfortune if anything were to happen to Thomas.

(During **Mrs. Moodie'***s spirited recitation the sleeper in the bunk at the right has awakened; first a hand appears, feeling the curtains; then a pair of bare legs appear over the side, and a girl steps to the floor. She wears a short coarse shift, and her hair hangs loose. She is a little weak when first she stands, but gains strength; she looks with curiosity into the cradle, then at the chest of drawers and into the mirror over it; then, slowly, she pulls on a draggled skirt which she gets from the bed, and a soldier's scarlet coat, which is too big for her, though not farcically so. She squats by the cradle and examines the baby; she then begins to rock it, crooning softly, but enough to be heard by the women on the other side of the curtain.)*

Mrs. Traill: Did you say that all the children had gone into Peterborough, Frances?

Mrs. Stewart: Yes, the day before yesterday. Why do you ask?

Mrs. Traill: I am mistaken, of course, but I thought I heard a child's voice singing.

Mrs. Stewart: I do not know how that could be, do you?

Mrs. Traill: No, though I am not usually deceived. Indeed, I pride myself that my hearing is uncommonly good.

Mrs. Stewart: Yes, my dear, I know that you do. More toast?

Mrs. Moodie: Yes. You really ought not to tease us in this way, Frances. The rebellion has made us all very edgy.

Mrs. Stewart: And very curious?

Mrs. Moodie: No curiosity about it. Mine is an open nature; I detest mysteries — particularly other people's. We are aching to know who is behind that curtain.

Mrs. Traill: Is it anyone we know?

Mrs. Stewart: I don't think so. I don't know her myself. Wait a moment. *(She goes through the curtain.)*

Mrs. Stewart: You are stirring! Is that really wise, my dear? Ought you not to lie down?

The Girl: Ah, sure, I'm fine.

Mrs. Stewart: But do you not feel weak and ill? Are you not light-headed?

The Girl: No, I'm fine.

Mrs. Stewart: But you must be hungry. You must have breakfast at once. And I may as well draw this curtain; it's no longer wanted.

*(She does so, and **Mrs. Moodie** and **Mrs. Traill**, who have been listening with keen interest, see the stranger.)*

Mrs. Moodie: So there's your redcoat! Frances, how you love to torment us all!

Mrs. Traill: Who is she?

Mrs. Stewart: You know quite as much as I do. Who are you, my girl?

The Girl: Honour. *(She curtsies.)*

Mrs. Stewart: Honour who?

The Girl: Honour Brady, I'm thinking. *(She curtsies again.)*

Mrs. Stewart: I don't recall that name. Do you live hereabout?

Honour: A piece up the river.

Mrs. Moodie: Brady? Any connection of old Phelim Brady?

Honour: Ah, sure, that's himself.

Mrs. Stewart: I know him; is he your father?

Honour: Well, in a queer kind of way you might say he was.

Mrs. Stewart: And does he know about your child?

Mrs. Traill: Child!

(She darts across the room, quickly followed by **Mrs. Moodie,** *and they gaze with interest into the cradle.)*

Honour: He does that.

Mrs. Stewart: My poor girl! Was he very angry with you?

Honour: No; what way would he have a right to be angry?

Mrs. Stewart: But you are unmarried?

Honour: Well, just at the present.

Mrs. Stewart: But have you some hope that you may be married?

Honour: Ah, sure, just the minute herself's buried.

Mrs. Moodie: This is a remarkably fresh-appearing infant. When was it born?

Mrs. Stewart: At four o'clock this morning in that bed.

Mrs. Moodie: That's as fresh as anyone could desire. And you were midwife, I presume.

Mrs. Stewart: I was.

Mrs. Moodie: And I see you on your feet, Honour, and ready for anything. That's nimble, even for Douro.

Mrs. Stewart: It was an easy birth, I must say.

Honour: Oh, I took my measures. I didn't want you to be destroyed with me screaming and roaring, so I drank a full pint of gin as soon as I felt me pains, and hurried here while I could still see out o' me eyes.

Mrs. Moodie and Mrs. Traill: *GIN!*

Honour: It's the best thing for a delivery there is. You never feel a qualm, and when the baby comes it'll sleep like Moses for half a day or so. It gives you a chance to get on your feet and start your milk, so.

Mrs. Traill: I never cease to marvel at the infinite adaptability of Nature.

Mrs. Moodie: Nature never framed anything more indestructible than the Irish settler. Behold Nature's masterwork — in the ironmongery line!

Honour: Sure, you've no call to say that! Didn't the cholera take me father and mother in a single day? The Irish are terrible delicate.

Mrs. Stewart: Did you not tell me that Brady was your father?

Honour: He brought me up since I was four.

Mrs. Stewart: This is becoming very confused. Please tell me more about yourself, and perhaps I shall be able to help you. Now, Brady is your foster-father?

Honour: He is that.

Mrs. Stewart: He knows that you are having a child?

Honour: He does that.

Mrs. Stewart: And you say that he is not angry?

Honour: Little good it would do him to be angry.

Mrs. Stewart: And is there any hope that the father of this child will marry you?

Honour: And isn't his own sainted wife after telling him he must?

Mrs. Stewart: Oh dear! Please don't confuse me any more. Whose wife?

Honour: Old Phelim's wife. "Marry her," says she, "as soon as the breath has passed from me body."

Mrs. Stewart: You mean that this is Brady's child?

Honour: You'd best sit quiet and let me explain. You're getting yourself all confused. Brady's wife took a creeping inflammation of the tubes of the head a year ago, and she knew her time was near. So she told himself that when she was gone he was to marry me, to have someone to look after him, you see. So he promised he would, and from time to time after that he sought my companionship as I was living handy in the house as I'd done from a child. And in time herself died — six weeks ago it was — and as soon as she's out of the way we'll be married surely.

Mrs. Stewart: You mean, when a proper period of mourning is over?

Honour: I mean nothing of the kind. I mean that the priest that buries her will marry us that same day.

Mrs. Stewart: Not buried!

Honour: Brady had a disagreement with the priest because he wasn't as close married to herself as he might have been. There's some ugly talk that she might have been a Protestant. But the Protestants'll have nothing to do with it, and the priest won't bury her at all. So Brady puts the corpse out on the roof the way the wolves won't get at it, and sits down to wait the whole lot of 'em out. He's a lucky old divil, for the frost has been strong ever since, and the priest is weakening. We'll be married by Christmas.

Mrs. Traill: In all my time in the backwoods I do not think that I have ever heard a more horrible tale!

Honour: The horrible part has still to be told. Phelim didn't want me to come here last night. "Stay snug in your bed," says he. "What," says I, "and bring forth the child with herself that was like a mother to me above on the roof friz as stiff as a cedar log? Sure, I've a proper regard for the feelings of the dead if you have none," says I, "and I'll not affront her with such bold behaviour." So I lowered the gin down me gullet as I told you, and came straight here, for it's well known, ma'am, that you turn nobody from your door. *(She curtsies to* Mrs. Stewart.*)*

Mrs. Stewart: Well Honour, I suppose that there is nothing for me to say except that the delicacy of your feelings does you credit.

Honour: Thank you, ma'am. Her that brought me up gave me a notion of what was owing to a corpse that Queen Victoria herself wouldn't better.

Mrs. Stewart: And what do you propose to do now?

Honour: Sure I don't know. Would I do right to go back?

Mrs. Traill: Oh no! You cannot take a child to a house where there is a body on the roof!

*(*Mrs. Stewart *gives* Honour *a generous hunch of bread and a cup of tea.)*

Mrs. Moodie: Catherine, I advise you not to concern yourself in this matter unless you are ready to make yourself responsible for the child in some degree. And as you already have as many children of your own as you can manage that would be an extremely rash undertaking.

Mrs. Traill: Susanna dear, sometimes you assume the tone almost of an elder sister. Pray permit me to decide on my own course of conduct.

Mrs. Moodie: I meant only to be kind, Catherine.

Mrs. Traill: We must not allow kindness to make us peremptory and dictatorial, must we, dear? Let me hold the child.

(She fetches the child from the cradle.)

This is a bonny child, Honour, but you must shape its head a little. I shall show you what to do. You must hold the child on your lap like this, and roll its head very gently between your palms, thus.

Mrs. Moodie: Catherine, pray be cautious! You will addle the child's brains with your rolling and squeezing!

Mrs. Traill: I have done this with many settlers' children, Honour, and they all have uncommonly pretty heads. I may say that I am quite famous for my skill in this respect. You must not be fearful. Do this for a few minutes two or three times each day. Now you do it.

(Honour *takes the child and begins a somewhat heavy-handed and rapid imitation of what* **Mrs. Traill** *has done.)*

Honour: Is this the trick of it, ma'am?

Mrs. Moodie: O Gemini, Catherine, she's twisting its head like a doorknob! Stop, girl, before you are an unwitting infanticide!

Honour: Sure and what's that you're calling me, ma'am?

(She gives the head a dreadful jerk in her anxiety.)

Mrs. Traill: Don't meddle, Susanna. You know nothing of children.

Mrs. Moodie: I know enough to keep free of your bone-twisting tricks.

Mrs. Stewart: *(Who has rescued the baby from* **Honour.***)* Please! I helped the child into the world, and I shrewdly suspect that I shall be the one who cares for it and its mother. We shall shape its head later, Catherine, when it is a little more secure on its neck.

(She gives the child to **Mrs. Traill.***)*

And Susanna, can I not persuade you to take a little more toast? I am sure you need it. And tea, as well? Honour, I wish that you would lie down again. I am sure that you feel perfectly well, but it would really oblige me greatly if you would rest.

Mrs. Traill: The first three weeks is the time for this sort of work, I assure you, Frances. I know what I am doing.

Mrs. Moodie: I have some little reputation as a physician, and I assure you, Catherine, that you don't. Give me that child.

Mrs. Traill: No, give it to me.

Mrs. Moodie: Catherine, I must insist —

Mrs. Traill: Susanna, pray do not interfere —

(During the last few minutes **Phelim Brady** *has come on the scene from the woods, and he has been peering through the window. He is an elderly, but not decrepit, Irishman in breeches, stockings, and lace-up boots, a tightly buttoned coat, and a lamentable night-cap over which he wears a sorry top-hat. He has a shrewd and even noble face, framed in Galway whiskers, and he ranges in manner between Irish bard and lowest sort of shebeener. He taps on the window.)*

Phelim: What're yez doin' there with me infant child?

(All are startled by this interruption, but **Mrs. Moodie** *and* **Mrs. Traill** *continue to struggle in a well-bred fashion for the possession of the child.)*

Mrs. Moodie: Mercy on us! Who's that?

Honour: Sure, it's himself!

Mrs. Traill: Susanna, I really must protest against your assumption of authority —

Phelim: Come along now, all of yez! What kind of a game is that you're at, with your haulin' and draggin'? Open up now, and let me in!

Mrs. Stewart: It's Brady, come to fetch you, Honour.

Phelim: Make haste now, or I'll kick in your door!

Mrs. Stewart: Why is he in such a temper?

Mrs. Moodie: Drunk, I suppose!

Mrs. Stewart: Oh dear, I have never learned to manage drunken men.

Mrs. Moodie: Leave him to me. *(She goes to the door and calls through it.)* Brady!

Phelim: *(In imitation of her tone.)* Moodie!

Mrs. Moodie: What's that you say, Brady?

Phelim: What's that *you* say, Moodie?

Mrs. Moodie: You will gain nothing by impudence.

Phelim: Neither will you.

Mrs. Moodie: What do you want?

Phelim: I want to see me new-born infant, to kiss it on the brow and acknowledge me paternity in the sight o' God and in the face of all this world! Now what do *you* want?

Mrs. Moodie: I want an undertaking from you that if I let you in, you will behave in an orderly and respectful manner.

Phelim: You'll get no such promise from me, ye old petticoated grenadier, ye!

Mrs. Traill: *(Placidly massaging the child's head.)* I think he resents your peremptory manner, Susanna.

Mrs. Moodie: Catherine, this is not the time to pursue a family dispute.

Mrs. Stewart: Permit me to try what I can do. *(She goes to the door.)* Brady!

Phelim: *(Removing his hat and bowing toward her voice.)* God bless and protect you, Mrs. Stewart, ma'am. Is that yourself?

Mrs. Stewart: It is, Phelim. Will you behave yourself if I bring the child out to you?

Phelim: And how could I help meself from behavin,' before a lady such as yourself, ma'am? Wouldn't your very presence put behaviour on a skunk?

Mrs. Stewart: You know, Phelim, that Mr. Stewart is from home and that we are all unprotected women here, so I must have your word that you will not make any trouble.

Phelim: Sure, don't I know how unprotected you are, ma'am, and that heathen savage of a Sally this minute leapin' out the back door to hit me a clout with the skillet? She'd put the fear o' God into the divil, that one!

Mrs. Stewart: I'll not let Sally harm you if you are peaceable. Give me the child, Catherine.

(She takes it, opens the door and goes out to **Phelim.** *He has refreshed himself from a snuff box, and sneezes violently on the child.)*

Phelim: Bless you, ma'am, you know the feelings of a father. Is it a boy or a child?

Mrs. Stewart: A girl, Phelim, a seven-pound girl. I weighed her on the fish scales. She is rather sleepy now.

Phelim: Drunk, eh? Well, she'll wake and start her screechin' soon enough. Where's the mother?

Mrs. Stewart: You should really be ashamed of yourself, Brady. I shall ask Mr. Stewart to speak to you when he returns. You have behaved disgracefully toward that poor girl. She trusted you as a father.

Phelim: And hadn't she a right? Amn't I a father to her and to her child as well? Can good nature go further?

Mrs. Stewart: Oh Brady, you are incorrigible!

Phelim: *(With a wink.)* I am that. It's eatin' potatoes and goat's milk that does it.

Mrs. Stewart: Honour, you had better come out.

Phelim: Come out, me darlin.' I've somethin' for ye.

(**Honour** *comes slowly from the house.*)

Honour: What have ye for me, Phelim?

(*The ladies call him "Feelim," but* **Honour** *calls him "Failim."*)

Phelim: (*Rushing at her and kicking her spitefully several times in the rear.*) I've that for ye, ye great ugly baboon, ye idlin' away nine months to bring forth a scalded monkey of a girl! Oh, wait till I get ye home, me fine madam! I'll beat the divil out of yer lazy hide! I'll learn ye to breed girls! Sure, wouldn't herself that's dead and on the roof rip the soul-case out of ye if she could reach ye! A disgraceful daughter and the divil's own wife y've been to me!

Mrs. Stewart: Sally!! Sally!

(**Sally** *rushes from behind the house, and fells* **Phelim** *with a well-placed blow from her skillet.*)

Mrs. Stewart: Oh, thank you, Sally. What a dreadful scene! I do hope you haven't killed the poor man.

Mrs. Moodie: Poor man, indeed! A shocking old villain!

Mrs. Stewart: He couldn't be dead, could he?

Honour: It's little ye know o' the old divil to ask that. Sure, he'd live to spite the world.

Sally: Water make him talk. I get water.

(**Phelim** *groans.*)

Honour: The mention o' water's roused him. He can't bear to be wetted. (*She kneels and shouts in his face.*) Wake up, ye old conundrum! Aren't you a fright and a disgrace to the whole world!

Phelim: Honour! Honour, me girl!

Honour: Well now, are ye proud of yourself?

Phelim: What happened to me?

Honour: *(With gusto.)* Yez were rootin' me in the rump and I got mad and levelled ye with me fist, that's what happened to ye. And I'll do it again if ye don't mind yer eye.

Mrs. Stewart: Oh, Honour, what a dreadful story!

Phelim: Ye lie! Ye never had power in yer fist to smite me the way I been smote. I been struck by lightning.

Honour: Ye been struck by me right hand!

Phelim: By lightning, I tell ye! I can feel it still roarin' around in the heels of me boots. Oh, Mrs. Stewart ma'am, will ye give me a little sup o' something to put life back in me!

Mrs. Stewart: No, Phelim, I will not. Honour, go into the house at once and take the child with you. You must get up, Phelim, and you must go at once.

(Honour does as she is told.)

Phelim: And where am I to go, a poor lonely old man without a wife or a child to care for him at all?

Mrs. Moodie: You've changed your tune, Brady. You were bold as brass a few minutes ago.

Phelim: It wasn't meself that spoke, but the drink within me. Everyone knows I'm a humble poor man, and with good reason, too.

Mrs. Stewart: And whose fault is it if you are humble and poor, Phelim, when the other Irish settlers here-about are thriving and doing well for themselves?

Phelim: Sure, it's because they're thriving that I'm wretched.

Mrs. Traill: That doesn't make sense.

Phelim: Yet it does, ma'am, if I may so, and I can tell ye why.

Mrs. Stewart: Poor fellow, you look wretchedly. Would you like a cup of tea?

Phelim: I would that, ma'am, thank ye.

Mrs. Stewart: Sally, get him some tea.

Sally: Bad old man. You twist my skillet.

(She shows him the skillet with its neck badly bent, then she goes.)

Phelim: So that was the thunderbolt? Ah, this is a terrible, terrible country, where the savages fight with the likes o' them things.

(He moves himself painfully to a stump, and sits down to rub his head.)

Mrs. Stewart: Now Phelim, I'm not going to let Honour go home with you until you can tell me that your first wife is buried, and that you will marry her, and that you will promise to treat her well. You must give up drink and go to work.

Phelim: Them's terrible hard conditions. How can I go to work when nobody around here will let me work?

Mrs. Moodie: What nonsense! As if everybody in the place were not crying out for labourers!

Phelim: I'll have ye know that I'm no labourer.

Mrs. Moodie: And what are you then?

Phelim: It's yerself has a right to pity me and understand me, Mrs. Moodie, for I'm one of your own kind. I'm a story-teller.

(Sally puts a cup of tea into his hand.)

Mrs. Moodie: What do you mean, one of my own kind?

Phelim: Oh, you think yerself far above me, because you can read and write. But haven't I the art of a real Irish story-teller? Amn't I the latter-day heir o' the great bards and story-tellers of the old land? I know more than five-score stories and poems in English and in the old tongue too, and I can tell ye a story will pass away a whole night from dusk till dawn. And can't I make up a new song for a wake or a wedding as quick as the fiddler can play?

Mrs. Moodie: I do not see what that has to do with me.

Phelim: Ye can't see because you're too proud and ignorant to see. You and me is two branches o' the same old tree. Ah, sure, don't I know that you write for them maggyzines in Montreal and in England itself, and wouldn't I do the same if I could? But did ye ever have a hundred people hangin' on your lips and laughin' and cryin' as ye told them a great story? I have!

Mrs. Moodie: I am not a vain author, but I think that there is a difference between the productions of an educated and disciplined taste and a rigmarole of memorized fairy tales!

Phelim: How wise ye are! There's a big difference, and it's this: my poems and tales are rooted deep in a mighty past, and yours are the thin and bitter squeezings from the weary fancy of a heartsore woman.

(During the latter part of **Phelim's** *speech,* **Mr. Edmund Cantwell** *has entered at the back of the stage and has been listening. He is a handsome man, in the Byronic-Satanic fashion of the period, and his manner is that of a gentleman of fashion. He is about thirty-five, that is to say, he is of the generation of the three women whom he now greets. He is dressed in a mixture of backwoods garb and London fashion; his fine shirt is loosely bound at the collar with a silk cravat, but he may wear a skin cap, and a buckskin wamus, and his appearance is more decorative than that of a working settler.)*

Cantwell: Who speaks of a heartsore woman?

Mrs. Stewart: Oh, good morning. I don't think that we have met, have we?

Cantwell: You know that we have not met, madam, but I think you know who I am, just as I know who you are. But let us preserve the decencies, by all means: I am Edmund Cantwell, madam, at your service. *(He bows.)*

Mrs. Stewart: *(Curtsies in return.)* Of course, Mr. Cantwell. It is so difficult to know how one should meet these situations in this new land, isn't it? I am Mrs. Thomas Stewart, as you surely know. Mrs. Traill, you do not know Mr. Cantwell, I believe? Mrs. Moodie, I am sure that you have heard of Mr. Cantwell.

Mrs. Moodie: I am sure that everybody has heard of Mr. Cantwell.

Cantwell: That is an ominous remark, madam. Are you the heartsore woman to whom this ancient Hibernian made reference?

Phelim: What's that you're after callin' me?

Cantwell: Nothing to your discredit, my good fellow. I am an Irishman myself. You spoke of a heartsore woman; to which of these ladies did you refer?

Mrs. Moodie: Mr. Cantwell, I do not propose to be the subject of a conversation between you and this wretched creature.

Cantwell: Then it was you, Mrs. Moodie?

Mrs. Stewart: Did you come here for some purpose, Mr. Cantwell? I should not like to detain you if you have a great deal to do.

Cantwell: I am appreciative of your concern, Mrs. Stewart, but my business is with your husband. I want to hire a yoke of oxen and a man to drive them, if that is possible.

Mrs. Stewart: My husband is from home, sir. He has gone to York. And I do not think that you will easily get a yoke of oxen in this neighbourhood, or a man either. All the gentlemen have gone to York because of the rebellion, and all the other men are gathered in Peterborough to defend the town if the need should be.

Cantwell: Ah yes, the rebellion. I had forgotten it.

Mrs. Traill: That is more than most people can do, sir.

Mrs. Stewart: The Queen has asked all the gentlemen of Upper Canada to rally to the defence of the government of York; I am surprised that you did not hear the proclamation.

Cantwell: I heard it, madam, but upon consideration I decided to ignore it.

Mrs. Moodie: Are we to understand that you are on the side of the rebels, then?

Cantwell: If I were on their side I should be with Mackenzie now. No; in this dispute I am on nobody's side, and as I hope to leave Upper Canada soon I am in urgent need of a man and a yoke of oxen.

Mrs. Stewart: I am sorry, but there is none to be got here, Mr. Cantwell.

Cantwell: Are you anxious for me to be gone, Mrs. Stewart?

Mrs. Stewart: Why, no sir, I said nothing of the kind.

Cantwell: No, but I sense a certain hostility in your manner. You are, of course, too much of a person of breeding to make it plain; but in the station of life to which, I think I may say, we both belong, it is not necessary to labour these hints. Now as you cannot let me have a man for my work, may I enquire if you have any need of a man — a gentleman, here? In short, is Phelim Brady making a nuisance of himself?

Phelim: I am not, sir! Do you take me for some common settler?

Cantwell: No, the common settlers are better dressed, and better looking, and in every way superior to you.

Mrs. Stewart: Brady has been assuring us that he is far above the common run.

Phelim: And isn't a poet and a storyteller miles beyond and above them common fellows is diggin' the ground and pullin' out stumps?

Cantwell: That is a question which has been debated for some hundreds of years, Phelim. Take what comfort you can from this: if a poet and a story-teller is both good, and dead, he may be considered the equal or even the superior of ordinary, decent, successful men; but so long as he has the bad taste to remain alive the question will always be in dispute, and the odds will always be heavily against him.

Phelim: (*Crossing to* **Cantwell.**) Don't I know the bitter truth of that, your honour! In the old land, now, I could get a fine living; sure, the people were that wretched they'd be glad of a tale or a song to beguile them from hunger and the thoughts of death and injustice. But here the poorest ruffian of them all has his bit o' land, and his pig, maybe, and the ones with good arms and good heads on them is thrivin' so fast they never feel the need of a story at all. They're not the people I knew, God help them. They're a strange lot entirely, with the blush o' health on their cheeks and the maggot o' respectability in their brains. They're wantin' schools for their young ones, and for me it's "Get away wid ye, Phelim; don't be wastin' our time wid yer talk." Sure, as if talk wasn't the sacred breath of all the mystery and grandeur is in the world!

Cantwell: There is a period of struggle between poverty and affluence during which men feel no need for what you have to offer them, Phelim. And there is a sort of education which forgets that the mind needs not only to be polished, but oiled. I am still curious about the heartsore woman. *(He crosses to the ladies.)*

Phelim: Mrs. Moodie, ma'am, I shouldn't have made bold on ye, the way I did, but ye must see surely that a country that has no need for my stories has no need for yours. And now, I'll take Honour and me child and get away home.

Mrs. Stewart: No Phelim, you will not. I told you that Honour shall stay with me until your home is fit to receive her.

Phelim: Fit, is it! And what's it been since she came to it as a child, and her own father and mother dead with the cholera morbus?

Mrs. Stewart: You know very well what I mean.

Cantwell: Mrs. Stewart no doubt refers to your uncommon fashion of disposing of your dead, Phelim. It is oddities of conduct of that sort which gets poets and storytellers their bad name.

Phelim: I want me wife and me child. How can a poet live without a woman to tend him? This is a free country; I want me rights!

Mrs. Traill: Oh dear, when people begin to shout about their rights I always get a blinding headache.

Mrs. Stewart: If you want your rights, Phelim, you had better be careful. My husband parcels out the land in this settlement and I can't recall that he ever gave you any. You are a squatter and you have no right in law to your cabin or any bit of land hereabout. But I won't ask Mr. Stewart to be hard on you if you will do what I told you. Bury your dead: marry Honour: go to work.

Phelim: I won't do any of 'em.

Mrs. Stewart: Then go away and don't come here again.

Phelim: Be damned if I'll budge.

Mrs. Stewart: Oh dear — *(She begins to laugh.)*

Mrs. Moodie: I see nothing to laugh at, Frances.

Mrs. Stewart: No, my dear, I don't suppose you do.

Mrs. Moodie: I suggest that you ask Sally to drive him away.

Mrs. Stewart: No, no; that would be cruel.

Mrs. Traill: But you cannot remain here unprotected, with this man in a threatening mood.

Mrs. Stewart: I don't think he is so very dangerous.

Phelim: Go on. Despise me, the lot of ye, if it gives ye any pleasure. But I've more courage in me pocket than the lot of ye — yes or your savage woman o' the woods — have in all yer carcasses.

(He produces from an inner pocket a case-bottle.)

Mrs. Traill: Great Heaven! Strong drink.

Phelim: The strongest. Ye could cut this seventeen ways with holy water and it'd knock ye down still. I'll be roarin'! I'll be terrible!

Mrs. Traill: And not a man in miles!

Cantwell: You forget, Mrs. Traill, that I am at your service.

Mrs. Traill: No, Mr. Cantwell, I have not forgotten. But if you had the spirit of a man, you would be in York, ready to defend the government. I cannot regard your presence, sir, as a source of reassurance.

Cantwell: Nevertheless, madam, beggars can't be choosers, if you will excuse the bluntness of the observation. Now, if I may offer a suggestion, let us go inside the house, and talk this matter over. Phelim must remain here, for the present, as he refuses to go, and I have not yet had your instructions to remove him.

Mrs. Stewart: That certainly seems the best plan. Let us go in at once.

(They go into the cabin; at the door **Cantwell** *bows with great elegance as the ladies pass him;* **Mrs. Stewart** *acknowledges this courtesy with a nod and a smile, but the* **Strickland** *sisters are frosty.* **Phelim** *sits on his stump, and views his bottle morosely.)*

Mrs. Stewart: What a lot of trouble this has been. Honour, if you won't lie down, put the baby in the cradle and go and help Sally, will you? You may be here for a while, and you may as well make yourself useful. And do, for goodness' sake, bind up your hair.

Honour: Yes, Mrs. Stewart, ma'am. *(She goes to the kitchen.)*

Mrs. Stewart: Do sit down, my dears. And you too, Mr. Cantwell.

(He declines. Here **Sally** *and* **Honour** *set the table for three.)*

If you are to be our protector we musn't lessen your strength by making you stand. I know I am being foolish, but I will not send that girl and a newborn child home with that dirty old man. Probably what I am doing is quite illegal, but I know it is right.

Mrs. Traill: If it is right it cannot be illegal. One can only deal with people like that by telling them what is good for them, and seeing that they behave themselves accordingly.

Cantwell: That is the simple principle of government, madam, which has given rise to the regrettable revolution, in suppressing which all your husbands are at present engaged.

Mrs. Moodie: And it is an extremely good principle of government, particularly in a new country, where many settlers have more liberty, and more money, than they know how to employ.

Cantwell: May I suggest, Mrs. Moodie, that one's opinion on that matter is likely to depend upon whether one belongs among the rulers, or the ruled?

Mrs. Moodie: You may suggest what you like, sir. I was in this country before you came, and it appears that I shall be here after you have gone. I think I know what I am talking about.

Cantwell: Everybody thinks that, including the rebel Mackenzie.

Mrs. Stewart: Let us not talk of that now. What are we going to do about Honour, and Phelim, and the baby? I don't think we need detain you, Mr. Cantwell; Phelim will grow tired of waiting after a while, and he will be reasonable in the morning.

(But Phelim has been listening to the last speech or two outside the door, and now he shouts in defiance.)

Phelim: I'll not be reasonable! Ye're hard oppressors o' the poor, the lot o' ye! I'll set fire to your house, that's what I'll do!

Cantwell: I shall go if you wish it, of course, but you may find Phelim troublesome. Wouldn't it be the best plan to give him his girl and be rid of him?

Mrs. Stewart: No, I refuse to do any such thing. He will beat her, and that I will not have.

Cantwell: If I go, as you suggest, he may come in and take her by force. Could you prevent him?

Mrs. Stewart: Sally could prevent him.

Cantwell: He is a determined old man, but not a strong one. Sally is not what I should call a clean fighter. What if she kills him?

Mrs. Stewart: Oh dear, I never thought of that.

Mrs. Traill: It is a possibility.

Mrs. Moodie: If she hit him again with the skillet, it would be a certainty.

Phelim: *(Still at the door.)* Don't think I don't hear you, whispering within with himself. Sure, wouldn't your husbands be ravin' if they knew it was closeted close with himself ye were, and him the wickedest fella in Douro and some says he's the Devil himself!

Cantwell: You hear that?

Phelim: Hasn't he a wife that's never seen by daylight?

Cantwell: You hear these terrible accusations?

Mrs. Stewart: He seems to be very wild. Perhaps you had better stay for a time, sir, if you will. What do you think, my dears?

Mrs. Moodie: I have no fear of that drunken old man, but there may be some unpleasantness, and I suppose we should avoid it if we can.

Mrs. Traill: I must say frankly, Mr. Cantwell, that what I know of you does not recommend you as a protector, but I agree with my sister.

Cantwell: Indeed, Mrs. Traill? And what do you know of me?

Mrs. Traill: Only that you are a gentleman settler who has held a large piece of land for two years, and never worked any of it; that you have avoided all your neighbours; that Mrs. Cantwell appears not to wish to make the acquaintance of any of the ladies in the district, though there are many of her own station in life; that you appear to hold dangerously radical political opinions; and that you have not answered the Queen's call to defend the government of Upper Canada.

Cantwell: But you do not believe that I am the Devil?

Mrs. Moodie: Pray don't trouble yourself to be facetious, sir, we are not in a mood for nonsense.

Phelim: Beware, women; beware! He'll tempt ye! He'll have the smocks off ye! Didn't Barney Flynn see a goat fly out of his chimney last Hallowe'en?

Cantwell: Phelim is doing his best to warn you.

Mrs. Stewart: Mr. Cantwell, we must not be so ungracious as to ask you for protection and then treat you rudely. If you will stay with us for a short time, we shall be most grateful, and I hope that you will join us in our midday meal?

Cantwell: With the greatest pleasure.

Mrs. Stewart: Sally!

(Sally comes in from the kitchen.)

Is the dinner almost ready?

Sally: Uh-hunh.

Mrs. Stewart: Lay a plate for Mr. Cantwell, will you?

Sally: Uh-hunh.

Mrs. Stewart: And will you be as quick as you can? We have had a rather trying morning.

Sally: *(emphatically)* Uh-hunh!

Cantwell: If any of you have the slightest objection to eating with the Devil, I shall be happy to take my plate out on the step. I should not wish to put you needlessly in the way of temptation.

Mrs. Moodie: You may be assured, sir, that if any of us are to be tempted, it will not be by you.

Cantwell: *(emphatically)* I have received your assurance, madam, and I shall treat it with all the respect it deserves.

Mrs. Stewart: Temptation is a word I have almost forgotten, except in my prayers, of course. Here in the backwoods temptation seems very far away.

Mrs. Traill: That is one of the very few things that can be said for the backwoods. I have remarked upon it often: the backwoods offer, as positive advantages, an unlimited supply of plant and animal life for scientific study, and a complete absence of temptation.

Mrs. Stewart: Oh I shouldn't say that, my dear. Look how many men succumb to the temptation of strong drink.

(By a gesture she indicates **Phelim,** *though of course she cannot see him.)*

Mrs. Traill: I meant temptation of the sort to which a lady of gentle breeding and good education might conceivably fall prey.

Mrs. Stewart: Oh, that sort of temptation.

Cantwell: You make yourself sufficiently clear, madam. I have been warned.

(By this time **Sally** *and* **Honour** *have set the table.)*

Mrs. Stewart: Shall we draw up our chairs to the table? Mr. Cantwell, will you sit on my right?

(Mrs. Moodie has already taken this position of honour for herself and with polite malice Cantwell places another chair for her.)

Cantwell: It is an honour, Mrs. Stewart.

Mrs. Stewart: Susanna, will you say one of your beautiful graces?

(All stand, but Cantwell does not close his eyes.)

Mrs. Moodie: Oh, Lord, who hast guided our steps thus far through the day, enable us to walk without sin toward the night. Consecrate this food to our use and bless us, thy loving servants.

Mrs. Steward and Mrs. Traill: Amen.

(Mrs. Stewart takes the lid off a fine silver dish, and an appetizing steam arises. Honour and Sally are in attendance.)

Phelim: *(Peering through the window.)* B'god, it's the Family Compact sittin' down to their food! And where's the common people? Out in the cold, every time; out in the cold! Hurrah for Mackenzie and responsible government!

(As the curtain falls, he takes a hefty swig from his bottle.)

(Curtain)

Act Two

(When the curtain rises it is plain that dinner has been over for some time, but the ladies and their guest are still seated around the table, and their high spirits are in marked contrast to what they showed at the end of Act One. **Phelim** *still sits in the dooryard, gloomy and disgruntled.)*

Cantwell: I really must stop talking. I have been monopolizing the conversation abominably.

Mrs. Stewart: On the contrary, sir, I hope that you will continue, for I have not been in such good spirits since my husband went to York.

Mrs. Traill: I have often reflected that the conversation of ladies alone is like a peal of bells without the support of the great bell; it readily becomes a clangour.

Cantwell: You are hard upon your sex, madam. You cannot conceive what pleasure it gives me, in this backwoods place, to hear my native tongue spoken with so much of that charm and delicacy which only ladies can impart to it.

Mrs. Moodie: You flatter us, Mr. Cantwell, upon a point which is very near to our hearts. We hear the Yankees, and the Irish, and many good, humble people, but it is rarely that we hear English spoken in a fashion that recalls the society to which we were accustomed in our better days.

Cantwell: Better days, madam?

Mrs. Moodie: Earlier days, I should have said.

Cantwell: But you think of them as better days, and you are right to do so. Your fashion of treating a guest, Mrs. Stewart, speaks eloquently of the Ireland which we both know.

Mrs. Stewart: When were you last in Ireland, sir?

Cantwell: A month less than two years ago I was the guest of Lord Rossmore.

Mrs. Stewart: Rossmore? You know him well?

Cantwell: Intimately. I think we have other friends in common. The Wallers and the Beauforts have spoken of you; Miss Edgeworth also honours me with her friendship.

Mrs. Moodie: Maria Edgeworth? How I envy you!

Cantwell: She sends all her new books to at least one friend in Upper Canada, for she told me so herself.

Mrs. Moodie: Yes, to Frances. We all read them greedily. They are a breath of a greater world to us here. We have little enough time to read, but half an hour now and then gives the mind something to feed on during the endless hours of sewing, mending, cooking, candle-making, preserving, gardening — all the tasks that devour our time in this Ultima Thule of civilization.

Cantwell: It is, indeed, a demanding life. So much so that I am giving it up. And if I may say so, I think that many others might be wise to give it up, as well.

Mrs. Stewart: There are many others who cannot give it up, sir.

Mrs. Moodie: And many who would be too proud to do so.

Cantwell: It is well to rid oneself of the folly of being too proud to do what is sensible.

Mrs. Traill: You are probably aware, sir, that our husbands are retired officers, who have their way to make in the world.

Cantwell: And who are trying to make it as farmers upon land which has not been farmed before, without previous knowledge of farming. That is very hard.

Mrs. Traill: You may well say so.

Cantwell: I have watched some of those officers here in Upper Canada following the plough, and whenever they rest — which it must be said to their eternal credit is rarely — they always come to a halt facing east. I think that without knowing it they are looking toward England, as they wipe the sweat from their brows.

Mrs. Traill: I would rather not talk about it.

Cantwell: Forgive me, I had not realized —

Mrs. Stewart: *(Bridging the difficult moment.)* I have a guilty conscience about Phelim. He must be growing very cold. I'll take him a cup of tea.

Mrs. Moodie: But Frances, you are punishing Phelim for his wickedness and trying to bring him to a better frame of mind. How can you do that and give him cups of tea at the same time.

Mrs. Stewart: Set it down to Irish irrationality, Susanna.

Cantwell: It is the sort of irrationality which makes our system of government endurable. If we will not permit people to run their own affairs, we are obliged to be very kind to them to make up for it.

Mrs. Stewart: If you will spare me any further philosophical observations and pithy generalities, I shall take Phelim his tea now.

Cantwell: I most humbly ask your pardon, madam.

Mrs. Stewart: Pray do not; I like your conversation very much. I thoroughly enjoy having a gentleman about the place to moralize and utter weighty apophthegms while I do as I please.

Cantwell: I shall accompany you.

Mrs. Traill: And I. I feel the want of air.

Mrs. Moodie: I shall come too. I want to see how the man who called me a petticoated grenadier is enduring the cold.

(During these speeches they have gone out-of-doors.)

Mrs. Stewart: Phelim, I have brought you a cup of tea.

Phelim: Is it gentry tea, or common folks' tea?

Mrs. Stewart: It is the last of the pot and strong enough even for you, I think.

Phelim: I don't know as I ought to take it.

Mrs. Stewart: Do, and oblige me. It is very hot.

Phelim: Well, if it's to oblige you, ma'am, I don't mind draining it through me, but don't think it'll soften me heart.

(During this, **Sally** *and* **Honour,** *indoors, clear the table.)*

Mrs. Stewart: I'm sure it won't but if you are determined to stay here I cannot allow you to freeze to death at my door.

Phelim: How wise ye are! Himself would skelp ye if ye treated me bad. I'll be waitin' here till he comes.

Mrs. Stewart: Compose yourself for a long wait, then, for I do not expect Mr. Stewart for many days.

Phelim: He's away to fight the revolution, I suppose?

Mrs. Stewart: Yes.

Phelim: A big help he'll be, and him with that delay in his right leg. There'll be great times in York, I'm thinkin,' and all them fine fellas there spoilin' for a fight. I wish to God I was with 'em. Sure there's no time like wartime for larkin.' Drunk every day before noon they'll be.

(He pours a generous dollop from his bottle into the hot tea, and drinks it at a gulp.)

Cantwell: And which side would you favour, Phelim, if you were there?

Phelim: The side the bards has always been on — both sides at once. Sure, I'd make songs o' victory for the conquerors, and take a sup with them, and I'd fashion laments for the vanquished, and take a sup with them. It's what ye call the impartiality o' the artist — rejoice and mourn with everybody and hit both sides a good clout if ye can.

Cantwell: Your philosophy of art differs from Mrs. Moodie's. She has written vigorously in support of the government side.

Phelim: The gentry ladies are all on the government side. The Queen's proclamation was hardly dry before Moodie and Traill were squeezin' themselves into their old uniforms, and scourin' up their swords with sand, and shoutin' around in hoarse voices the way ye'd think the trees was all sojers. Hasn't this revolution been a glory and a blessed gift to them! Back to sojerin,' and away from this cursed spot, and away from their wives and their debts. They've a right to be yellin' for the revolution, I'm tellin' yez!

Cantwell: You should not speak so before Mrs. Moodie and Mrs. Traill.

Mrs. Moodie: Let him say what he pleases. He is railing so bitterly because he is on the losing side in the little battle that is being fought right here.

Phelim: Go on! Pity me if it does ye good! But I told you this morning, me fine madam, and I tell ye again that you and me is both in one losin' battle. We're the songbirds that aren't wanted in this bitter land, where the industrious robins and the political crows get fat and they with not a tuneful chirp among the lot of 'em!

Mrs. Traill: How odd that poets are such bad naturalists! There are songbirds all about you, you foolish old man! Come Susanna, I am going inside. It is colder than I thought, and you have no shawl, my dear.

Mrs. Moodie: Phelim, if you think to hurt me, you must use a hickory club. I am an author, and I have winced under the lash of professional criticism. Words are powerless upon me.

(She and her sister go into the house.)

Cantwell: Shall we follow them?

Mrs. Stewart: Just a moment, Mr. Cantwell; I want a few more moments in the sunshine. Shall we walk in this direction?

Phelim: Ah, ye want to say somethin' them two mustn't hear.

(They ignore him, and walk to the right, out of his earshot.)

Mrs. Stewart: It embarrasses me to find that we have friends in common, Mr. Cantwell. I feel that I have been shamefully rude and neglectful toward you and your wife. I should have called upon her many months ago.

Cantwell: There is no cause for embarrassment, I assure you. We did not show ourselves friendly. I presume that you know why that was so?

Mrs. Stewart: I know nothing about it.

Cantwell: You heard the rumours about us, surely.

Mrs. Stewart: I pay no attention to rumours.

Cantwell: But in this case the rumour was the truth. Mrs. Cantwell was a novice in a nunnery in Cork. She was forced into that position because her parents did not want her to marry me. I rescued her, and brought her here. She was not anxious to meet many people for some months. But now we are returning to Europe.

Mrs. Stewart: To Ireland?

Cantwell: To Italy.

Mrs. Stewart: If it had been to Ireland I should have asked you to take some messages to friends there.

Cantwell: To Miss Edgeworth?

Mrs. Stewart: To her, of course; and to Lord Rossmore.

Cantwell: Rossmore travels a great deal; I may well see him on the Continent. What shall I tell him?

Mrs. Stewart: *(after some hesitation)* Oh, give him my good wishes.

Cantwell: Nothing more?

Mrs. Stewart: What more should there be?

Cantwell: I knew Rossmore intimately. Not long before I left Ireland we were together in a day's hunting. He was thrown from his mount at a rather dangerous leap, and when he did not rise at once I feared that he might have broken his neck. There were no others near, and I knelt to examine him; his pulse beat faintly, and I opened his shirt to listen to his heart. Around his neck, on a chain, was a locket; in it was a lock of hair and a miniature of a beautiful young woman.

Mrs. Stewart: You opened it?

Cantwell: I did, madam.

Mrs. Stewart: Was not that a breach of confidence?

Cantwell: No; it was a friendly precaution. If he had been dead I should have removed the locket at once. For the portrait was not that of Lady Rossmore. Men do such things for one another, you know.

(Pause.)

Mrs. Stewart: Do you tell that story to many chance acquaintances?

Cantwell: I have never told it to anyone but yourself, for you alone have the right to know it.

Mrs. Stewart: Why have you told it to me?

Cantwell: Because it piques my sense of the incongruous to know of this link between a world of brilliant fashion and the backwoods of Canada.

Mrs. Stewart: There is no link, I assure you.

Cantwell: With the best will in the world, madam, I do not believe you. Indeed, I have seen that picture; I cannot believe you.

Mrs. Stewart: Is my assurance nothing?

Cantwell: You gave stronger assurance of the truth of my suspicion when I mentioned Rossmore at the table. And there is more colour in your cheek now than you know. And can you deny that you asked me to remain here with you outside the house to quiz me about him? I am not a simple man, Mrs. Stewart; I can see through a brick wall with tolerable clarity.

Mrs. Stewart: If once there was a strong attachment between Lord Rossmore and me, you have no right to suggest that it endures still. I was curious about a former friend, that is all.

Cantwell: A friend who still cherishes your memory very dearly. Do not think that I imply anything discreditable to either of you, or injurious to Lady Rossmore, who is my friend, too. But when I see her once again in the midst of that brilliant and fashionable society, with the light of a hundred candles falling upon her jewels, shall I be able to repress a thought of you, sitting on a rush chair by the light of a backwoods fire?

(Far away the note of a horn is heard, clear and mysterious in the still December air.)

Mrs. Stewart: I do not know Lady Rossmore, nor do I envy her her jewels or her friends.

Cantwell: I am sure that you do not. And yet how well you would become such a life!

Mrs. Stewart: I? You are absurd.

Cantwell: No. You are beautiful, highly born, witty, and possessed of that wonderful generosity of spirit — that quality of *giving* — which raises beauty and charm to the level of great and holy virtues. What need has the backwoods of these things? You should not be here. You chose wrongly.

Mrs. Stewart: I cannot permit you to say more. Do not follow me.

(Agitated, she goes out left, passing **Phelim,** *who raises his head slightly.* **Cantwell** *watches her reflectively, and then goes into the house. His step is jaunty and he hums an Irish air under his breath.* **Mrs. Moodie** *and* **Mrs. Traill** *have been unobtrusively busy during the previous scene;* **Mrs. Traill** *has been by the fire, peacefully knitting, and her sister has sat at the table, with her back to the audience, writing busily.)*

Mrs. Traill: You look glowing, Mr. Cantwell; the air has done you good. Where is Frances?

Cantwell: Mrs. Stewart has gone for a walk, madam, and she did not care for my company.

Mrs. Traill: A walk? That is strange, at this time of day.

Cantwell: I understand that she shares your enthusiasm for the study of nature, Mrs. Traill. Perhaps she has gone in search of specimens.

Mrs. Traill: *(laughing)* Mr. Cantwell, what a droll notion! What specimens, as you call them, would she find in December?

Cantwell: I cannot say. I am utterly ignorant of such things.

Mrs. Traill: So it appears, sir.

Cantwell: But not so ignorant that I have not heard of your fame as a naturalist, madam.

Mrs. Traill: My fame is little enough. If my fame were equal to my enthusiasm, I might have cause to boast.

Cantwell: No, fame is what I said, and fame is what I meant. When I first arrived in this country I met a Mr. Sheppard in Quebec who, when he found that I was coming to this part of the backwoods, urged me particularly to seek your acquaintance.

Mrs. Traill: I know Mr. Sheppard only through correspondence.

Cantwell: So he told me. But he said that your letters revealed a quite extraordinary scientific capacity.

Mrs. Traill: This is flattering, and I wish it were true. Mr. Sheppard is preparing a book on Canadian flora, and I was able to give him some trivial assistance in describing the great wealth of plants and flowers which we find hereabout.

Cantwell: He told me that he had asked you to be one of three or four expert collaborators in the preparation of that work.

Mrs. Traill: Yes, he paid me that great compliment, but I did not think that I was worthy of it, although I did what I could.

Cantwell: You had other work of course, which made such a collaboration out of the question.

Mrs. Traill: That is true. The wife of a settler has no trifling day's work, as I am sure you know.

Cantwell: Was that not a pity, madam?

Mrs. Traill: I do not understand you, sir. I see nothing pitiful about my life. Quite the contrary; it is filled with interest. My excursions into natural science, when I have time for them, give me the greatest joy, I assure you.

Cantwell: I did not mean to suggest that there is anything pitiful about you as a person. But is it not a pity that so much of your time is absorbed in work which is not your proper concern?

Mrs. Traill: Really, Mr. Cantwell, you are still a stranger in Canada. No one is ashamed to do useful work here.

Cantwell: You wilfully misunderstand me. You are able to do work which no one else can do. Why should you waste your time in tasks of which any woman is capable?

Mrs. Traill: I do not consider this a profitable discussion.

Cantwell: I am being intolerably intrusive, I know. But I cannot bear to see genius wasted.

Mrs. Traill: *(Speaks quietly, but the arrow has found its mark.)* You abuse the word genius.

Cantwell: It is not my word, but Mr. Sheppard's. Do you know what he said to me, madam? "If Mrs. Traill could give all her time to her studies of natural life she could do for her part of Upper Canada what Gilbert White did for Selborne."

(For the second time the horn is heard, nearer but still distant. There is a pause while **Mrs. Traill** *considers what he has said.)*

Mrs. Traill: That was generous praise.

Cantwell: Tell me honestly; do you think it was too generous?

Mrs. Traill: Yes; it was quite ridiculous.

Cantwell: I asked you for an honest answer.

Mrs. Traill: What right have you to pry in this fashion?

Cantwell: If you have it in you to do notable scientific work it is not my concern, as a man of some education myself, to ask why you make it a bad second to the drudgery of a settler's wife?

Mrs. Traill: You do not understand what you are talking about. A new country brings hope, and it also demands sacrifice. Have you ever walked in our graveyard? Many stones there mark the graves of children. One of those children was — *is* mine. A fair hope vanished, Mr. Cantwell. And other hopes must be buried which may be even harder to give up. New countries mean not only hopes fulfilled but hopes relinquished. I must ask you not to try to estimate the claims of my duty to my husband and my children.

Cantwell: Are you sure that you know what your duty is? Mr. Traill is an estimable gentleman, but it is no secret that he is one of the least capable settlers hereabout. He was not framed for such work, and neither are you. As for your children, it might lie in your power to pass on to them a great name.

Mrs. Traill: Are you suggesting that my husband's concerns should play second fiddle to my work?

Cantwell: Aha, you have said it. Your *work*. Yes, madam, I am suggesting that for your sake, and your children's sake, and for the sake of the advancement of knowledge, your husband should play second fiddle to you.

Mrs. Traill: Do you see nothing immoral — nothing contrary to the law of nature, in such a proposal?

Cantwell: No, madam, and neither do you, in your heart of hearts. We are not animals, and the female does not live at the sufferance of the male.

Mrs. Traill: It is not my province, sir, to ask you to leave this house, and therefore I have no choice but to leave it myself. I shall go in search of Mrs. Stewart, and I hope that when I return you will no longer be here.

Cantwell: As you please, Mrs. Traill.

(She puts on her shawl, which she has kept close at hand since her first entrance, and goes out; she asks **Phelim** *which way* **Mrs. Stewart** *has gone, and he points out the direction; she goes the same way.* **Cantwell,** *meanwhile, turns his attention upon* **Mrs. Moodie,** *who has been listening to the past conversation, although she has kept up a pretence of her writing; she does not raise her eyes until he speaks. His approach to her is that of the intellectual bully, in*

contrast to his air of calm reason when talking to **Mrs. Traill,** *and the romantic air which he gave to his scene with* **Mrs. Stewart.***)*

Cantwell: I fear that I have discomposed your sister. But she is a remarkable woman pretending to be an unremarkable one, and that cannot be tolerated. Now you, Mrs. Moodie, are another remarkable woman, and you know it.

Mrs. Moodie: I have no wish for a private conversation with you, Mr. Cantwell. I shall call Sally.

Cantwell: Call her by all means, but do not forbid me to talk, for I shall certainly disobey you.

Mrs. Moodie: It is not in my power to gag you.

Cantwell: Nor would you, if you had the power. After hearing what I said to your sister you will not be content until you have heard my opinion of you. Who ever heard a sister praised without wishing to try her own luck?

Mrs. Moodie: You are impertinent, sir.

Cantwell: I have been told that I have the cheek of the Devil.

*(***Mrs. Moodie*** goes to the kitchen door, and calls.)*

Mrs. Moodie: Sally, Honour, what are you doing?

Honour: We're braiding rags, ma'am.

Mrs. Moodie: Bring your work in here, will you? I want company.

*(***Sally*** comes in, ill-pleased, and ***Honour*** follows with a basket of clean rags, some braided into long strips.)*

Sally: Not braid rags in best room. That kitchen work.

Honour: Ah, sit down and stop your talkin.' Don't ye see she has to have us here?

Sally: No.

Honour: Gentry ladies can't trust themselves alone with a man. They're that frisky they'd be at him at once. It's all the rich food they eat.

Mrs. Moodie: Honour, hold your tongue.

(**Honour** *and* **Sally** *sit on the floor and work during the scene which follows.*)

Cantwell: Did you disagree with Mr. Sheppard's estimate of your sister's abilities, Mrs. Moodie?

Mrs. Moodie: It is not a matter in which I am qualified to judge.

Cantwell: But Sheppard is, don't you agree?

Mrs. Moodie: Mr. Sheppard's opinion must be allowed a great deal of weight.

Cantwell: You felt, perhaps, that I pushed the matter too far?

Mrs. Moodie: I really have no views on the subject.

Cantwell: Perhaps I was wrong. After all, a woman's first duty is to her husband.

Mrs. Moodie: That is the accepted belief.

Cantwell: Even when it means the subordination of her own dearest wishes — perhaps of a very great talent.

Mrs. Moodie: Most people hold that opinion.

Cantwell: Your sister might achieve fame as a naturalist, perhaps, but it is unquestionably more important that Mr. Traill should make a farm in the wilderness.

Mrs. Moodie: (*Giving a ladylike snort.*) Hummph!

Cantwell: I scarcely know how to interpret that sound, madam. Was it intended as assent?

Mrs. Moodie: I think you know how much hope there is that any of us will make a fortune at farming.

Cantwell: Mr. Stewart seems very comfortably off.

Mrs. Moodie: Mr. Stewart brought money with him, and money begets money. To begin life here, as my sister and I have done, with all to seek, is to begin with the certainty of failure.

Cantwell: And yet many of the humbler settlers seem to be thriving.

Mrs. Moodie: They know how to work in a sense that my husband and Mr. Traill do not; my husband can plan and contrive better than they, but he has not the strength for twelve hours a day of back-breaking labour, every day of the week, month in and month out. What is more, many of these humbler settlers, as you call them, sponge on us shamelessly when they need help, and why? Because we are gentry, and so are obliged to give to the needy when we have not enough for ourselves. Gentle breeding brings obligations; when it does not also bring money the obligations may grow burdensome, but they cannot be thrown off. Because we are gentry we cannot live without a few of the comforts of life which the humbler settlers have not known and do not therefore miss. Those comforts make the difference between an endurable life and what we should consider degradation; they also make the difference between a very little profit on a year's work, and debt, debt, debt! Among the gentlefolk who have come to settle in this country, Mr. Cantwell, there are a few wastrels, but there are scores who have learned the bitter lessons that superior abilities may suffer the most complete frustration for the want of a few hundred pounds of capital! Good birth and gentle breeding carry with them tastes and obligations which are costly to maintain.

Cantwell: Was there no alternative?

Mrs. Moodie: There was life as a half-pay officer in England. You know what that is.

Cantwell: Poor Mrs. Traill!

Mrs. Moodie: Mrs. Traill?

Cantwell: Yes, were we not talking of Mrs. Traill? Sheppard says she is a genius buried in the forest. You apparently agree with her that she must remain buried. A great pity and the world's loss.

Mrs. Moodie: A woman's first duty is to her husband.

Cantwell: And the husband's first duty is to —

Mrs. Moodie: To his career, or to his destiny, I suppose.

Cantwell: And might not the woman's career, or destiny, sometimes be of greater importance? I have told your sister what one able scientist thinks of her. Come, Mrs. Moodie; you and I understand and appreciate these things better, perhaps, than most people. Because a husband's hope is blighted, must his wife's even greater hope be blighted too? Merely to spare his masculine vanity?

Mrs. Moodie: It is very, very hard.

Cantwell: Then I was right to press the matter to a conclusion with your sister?

Mrs. Moodie: It was unpardonably rude and intrusive, but I cannot say that it was wrong.

Cantwell: I felt that you would agree with me. After all we have somewhat the same cast of intellect.

Mrs. Moodie: You and I, sir?

Cantwell: Oh, do not imagine that I put myself on your level. You are a creator; I a critic. I once thought that I had some small talent as a writer, but it was too small for the company I kept. I was a friend of Byron, you know.

Mrs. Moodie: You knew Byron?

Cantwell: Yes, and most of his circle. I am glad to think that he sometimes asked my opinion of his verse. You did not suppose, did you, that Maria Edgeworth was the only literary person among my acquaintance?

Mrs. Moodie: I have long admired Miss Edgeworth. Of course, to someone who has known Byron —

Cantwell: Precisely. But I am sure that Miss Edgeworth should be proud of your good opinion.

Mrs. Moodie: Should be?

Cantwell: You are surely aware that your abilities are in no way inferior to hers.

Mrs. Moodie: I am not aware of anything of the kind, nor do I believe it. And what do you know of my abilities?

Cantwell: I have read many of your stories and verses in Montreal and New York journals. I think very well of them.

Mrs. Moodie: I am obliged to you. But you will hardly expect me to accept that as the approbation of Byron.

Cantwell: No, but there was a time when, young as I was, Byron did not despise my approbation.

Mrs. Moodie: I ask your pardon; I was rude. It is only that — you see, my situation is such that —

Cantwell: That you are unaccustomed to praise from your intellectual equals?

Mrs. Moodie: That I am unaccustomed to praise at all. I write, it is true, and I am paid for what I write, but I rarely hear any comment upon it. It is all hasty work, done when I am tired, and when I can snatch an hour from other, pressing tasks. I do it, I tell you frankly, because the money is sorely needed. That it should have any merit is more than I have dared to hope.

Cantwell: Madam, I would scorn to flatter you. Indeed, with a lady of your intellectual stature flattery would be useless. I do not say that you always write well. I say, rather, that your writing is that of one who might, under favourable circumstances, write very well indeed. How well I cannot say, of course, but I beg that you will cease to gaze upward toward Miss Edgeworth when it is fitting that you should look her in the eye.

Mrs. Moodie: I, the peer of Maria Edgeworth!

(The horn is heard for a third time, nearer but not too near.)

Cantwell: Yes, why not?

Mrs. Moodie: But I have never attempted a work of any length; I have had no opportunity to do so.

Cantwell: Ah yes; you are in your sister's position. You must play second fiddle to the incompetence of Lieutenant Moodie.

Mrs. Moodie: How dare you speak so!

Cantwell: How dare you, madam, pretend to me that wifely loyalty is more important than your very considerable talents as a writer!

Mrs. Moodie: You are impertinent.

Cantwell: Of course I am impertinent. People who care greatly for anything must be so. And I care greatly for your talent, which I know, and I have no concern whatever with the ambitions of your husband, whom I do not know.

Mrs. Moodie: You should not press this discussion; it is unmanly to take such advantage of me.

Cantwell: Humbug! You talk like a foolish girl being kissed in a corner. We are not man and woman, Mrs. Moodie, but artist and connoisseur — a vastly more delicate relationship — and I tell you that you may strangle all your children in their beds, murder Moodie with the cleaver, trample the British flag under your feet and Almighty God will find some mercy for you; but if you refuse, for an idiotic scruple, to write your best, He will put you into hell-fire and I, as a critic, will applaud His judgement. Do you understand me?

Mrs. Moodie: You make my scribbling seem very important.

Cantwell: Do you suppose that the importance of literature is diminished because nobody hereabout understands it? Would music cease to exist because your neighbours were deaf? I have said that Mrs. Traill's work is important. But that is science — a chilly business at best. Your work is art, and art is what gives form and meaning to life. Dare you neglect the sacred obligation which has been laid upon you?

(Mrs. Stewart and Mrs. Traill have returned, and as they pass Phelim he accosts them.)

Phelim: Mrs. Stewart ma'am, will ye have a little charity? I want my girl and my child, and if ye give me them two I'll go and not trouble yez any more.

Mrs. Stewart: Wait a moment, Phelim. I shall attend to you very soon. Are you cold?

Phelim: I'm perished, ma'am, and me rump's dyin' under me with the weight of the sittin' I've done.

Mrs. Stewart: Be patient for a few minutes longer.

(They go into the house and she addresses **Cantwell** *from the door.)*

Mrs. Stewart: Mr. Cantwell, I do not think that we need detain you any longer. Phelim is quite reasonable now. You have been most kind to help us during this rather troublesome time, and I am sure that you have much to attend to.

Cantwell: You are very kind, ma'am, but I cannot think of leaving until I have apologized to Mrs. Traill. I spoke unguardedly, and I am very sorry.

Mrs. Traill: It is of no consequence, I assure you.

Cantwell: I am glad that you see it in that way, ma'am. Now about Phelim — you know, of course, that once he has Honour out of this house he will beat her. Won't you Phelim?

*(***Phelim** *has been standing outside the door, and he falls into the trap at once.)*

Phelim: Indeed and I will, sir! I'll scoop the heart out o' her with me naked nails! Isn't she the bold, undutiful strumpet to be troublin' her betters and defyin' me that's been more than a father to her!

Honour: Are yez lookin' for another clout to match the one I gave ye this mornin'?

Phelim: Ye never hit me no clout, ye puny, sneakin' trollop! Don't I know 'twas the big savage struck me. Awww, won't I let the fresh air into yer hide!

*(***Sally**, *with an ancestral war-whoop, dashes through the door brandishing a hatchet which she has fetched from the kitchen, and puts* **Phelim** *to flight; but with sudden courage he turns upon her, his bottle held aloft.)*

Phelim: If ye strike me, watch out for me bottle. I didn't leave me native land to be domineered over by the likes of yourself.

Mrs. Stewart: Sally! Come into the house at once! How dare you!

Sally: I no kill, only scare. Wicked old man.

(She trots obediently indoors and to the kitchen, giggling. **Cantwell** *closes the door at once, and* **Phelim** *is left the master of the dooryard.)*

Phelim: Go on, me lady! Keep me from what's me own, if ye dare! When himself returns I'll have me say.

(He advances upon **Mrs. Stewart** *with drunken menace; when she rushes to safety in the house he sits defiantly again upon his stump, and refreshes himself from his bottle.)*

Cantwell: As I was saying, once Phelim has Honour out of your sight, he will beat her. However, I dare say she's used to it. Aren't you, Honour?

Honour: Ye never get used to beatin.' That's something only them thinks that's never been bet.

Cantwell: And there is, of course, the delicate situation involving the corpse of the late Mrs. Brady.

Mrs. Stewart: Oh, what a vexing position to be in!

Cantwell: I sympathize with you. But I do not think that we can discuss it thoroughly in front of Honour.

Mrs. Stewart: Go into the kitchen, Honour, and see to your child. How is she?

Honour: Och, fine — fine. I don't suppose anybody'd see it but me, but d'ye know she's a kind of an honest-lookin' little crature. *(She goes.)*

Mrs. Stewart: Honour will be a good mother. But what will the honest-lookin' little crature do when she comes to know her father?

Cantwell: Mrs. Stewart, and ladies, I know that my presence here is an embarrassment to you.

Mrs. Stewart: That is very frankly stated, Mr. Cantwell.

Cantwell: I assure you that I have no wish to prolong that embarrassment for one moment longer than is needful. But if I leave you here alone, what will you do if Phelim becomes troublesome?

Mrs. Moodie: Sally has twice shown herself more than a match for Phelim.

Cantwell: Do you intend to keep the girl here indefinitely?

Mrs. Stewart: Until my husband returns. He will know what to do.

Cantwell: When do you expect him?

Mrs. Stewart: I do not know. But we shall be perfectly safe.

Phelim: *(who has been brooding upon his wrongs)* Ye're a pack o' female blackguards! It'd serve ye right if I set fire to your roof!

Cantwell: You hear that?

Mrs. Stewart: It's nothing but wild talk.

Cantwell: It is a kind of wild talk which has grown into wild action in more than one backwoods settlement since the revolution began in York. I must remind you that to Phelim and people like him you settlers of the privileged class have begun to appear as oppressors. What if he collects a gang of ruffians and gives you real trouble?

Mrs. Traill: Oh, please don't suggest such a thing. He may be listening at the door.

Mrs. Stewart: We know the risks as well as you, Mr. Cantwell. But I ask you to go.

Cantwell: Better danger than my society: is that it?

Mrs. Stewart: I entreat you, if you have any gentlemanly feeling, to go at once!

Cantwell: Very well, I shall go. But before I go I beg you to permit me to say how very sorry I am that I have disturbed you all so profoundly.

Mrs. Moodie: You have disturbed my sister, sir. You have not touched me.

Mrs. Traill: Oh, no, Susanna; it is Frances who has been disturbed.

Mrs. Stewart: What you have said to me, sir, is of no consequence. But you have taken intolerable liberties with Mrs. Traill.

Cantwell: I assure you madam, that was not my intention. But it is clear that I have given offence by suggesting to you all three that you are wasted in the backwoods. It was an unpardonable liberty, and I beg your forgiveness.

Mrs. Stewart: Let us say no more about it.

Cantwell: Certainly not. No such hint shall ever pass my lips again.

Mrs. Stewart: I am sure that you spoke hastily.

Cantwell: I spoke from the best feeling that was in me. Listen to me, I entreat you, and then judge me how you will. Here in the forest I meet a lady whom a poet might adore for her charm, her beauty, and her loveliness of spirit! I meet another gifted with power to see into the very heart of Nature herself and to reveal the mysteries of Nature to mankind: and as though this were not adventure enough for a single day, I meet still a third whom I know to be capable of enriching the world through acts of creation no less miraculous than the miracle of life itself. I find these three Graces hidden in the wilderness. Should I remain silent? Would you ask me to close my lips if I saw Pegasus toiling at the plough? No! I spoke. I said what lay in my heart. But it was not in that alone that I offended. My transgression was that I said what lay in your hearts, and you cannot forgive me.

Mrs. Moodie: You have little regard for duty, sir.

Cantwell: I have told you, madam, where your real duty lies.

Mrs. Stewart: I refuse to hear you.

Cantwell: But you will always hear what your heart tells you. I have spoken your unacknowledged feelings; they will never be without a voice again.

Mrs. Stewart: Please, please, please do not torture me!

Mrs. Traill: Frances, what do you mean?

Mrs. Stewart: Forgive me; but I think his words have deeper meaning for me than for you.

Mrs. Traill: Can you imagine that I hear him without some pain?

Cantwell: I do not seek to cause you pain. I beg you only to come back to the world which is rightfully yours, and which has a place for you.

Mrs. Moodie: You have caused us all pain.

Cantwell: I have done nothing but give words to the pain which you have long felt. And it is so shameful? Is it a thing to keep hidden? Do not many settlers feel a kindred pang? Only a few weeks ago my eye was caught by some verses which an unhappy settler had sent to the Cobourg paper. Rough and simple as they were they captured a feeling common enough here. I recall a few lines.

(He recites with deep pathos, and the last defences of the ladies are broken.)

> I canna ca' this forest home,
> It is nae home to me;
> Ilk tree is suthern to my heart
> And unco' to my e'e.
> I canna ca' this forest home,
> And in it live and dee;
> Nor feel regret at my heart's core,
> My native land for thee.

Mrs. Stewart: It is utterly impossible that any one of us should admit the truth of what you have said.

Cantwell: I wish for your sakes that that were so, but you have admitted it already — at your heart's core.

*(There is a lively fanfare on a bugle offstage, and the **Hon. Thomas Stewart** enters; he is a man of kindly, merry appearance, dressed like a gentleman, but with heavy boots and strains of travel. He is lame in his right leg, and limps, using a heavy stick whenever he moves. From this instant the scene changes character sharply, and moves rapidly to its climax.)*

Stewart: Phelim, you rascal, what are you doing here? I've some news for you! Hello, there! Anybody at home? Nobody here to greet the survivor of the rebellion? Frances! Frances!

(Mrs. Stewart and the ladies have risen in haste, and with obvious relief they unbar the door and rush into the dooryard to greet him.)

Mrs. Stewart: Thomas! Dearest! Oh, I am so happy to have you back! *(She embraces him, weeping.)*

Stewart: What's this? Tears? What's amiss, my pet? Eh?

Mrs. Traill: Mr. Stewart! What joy to see you! Have you news for us?

Mrs. Moodie: I am rejoiced to see you, sir. The rebels, I presume, have been dispersed?

Stewart: Weren't you expecting me? I left Joseph and the waggon in Peterborough, and I've been sounding my bugle ever since, in the hope that someone might come to meet me.

Mrs. Stewart: Oh, Thomas! I heard nothing.

Stewart: I declare, Frances, that's the first time you've ever failed to hear my bugle. Is anything wrong?

Mrs. Stewart: No, nothing; nothing at all. It's just that I am so happy to have you back.

Stewart: Oh, come; you haven't been fretting have you? I was never in the least danger. But you all three look devilish queer. What's been amiss here?

Phelim: Aha, wouldn't ye like to know, your honour. As if the three noble dames hadn't been closeted with a strange man since before noon.

Stewart: What? What's this, Frances? Who's been here?

Mrs. Stewart: It is nothing of any consequence, Thomas, believe me.

Mrs. Moodie: Pay no attention to that man. He's drunk.

Phelim: *(Hopping up on his stump.)* Not so drunk that I couldn't see what palaverin' and whisperin' and runnin' out o' the house cryin' there's been this day. Did ye think I hadn't got me eye peeled, me fine ladies? Didn't I tell ye I'd have somethin' to say to himself when he came home?

Stewart: Phelim, be silent! If there is anything that I should know, my dear, let us go inside and I shall hear it.

(Cantwell comes to the door of the house; his manner is sharply changed to an air of arrogant contempt and amusement.)

Cantwell: There is no need for a long explanation, Mr. Stewart; I can tell you all there is to know in a few words. A few hours ago these three ladies boasted to me that there was no temptation in the forest. Since that time I have tempted them, all three, and with complete success!

(Curtain)

"Hot Codlings" *(Musical score)*

Act Three

(When the curtain rises, the day has grown perceptibly darker, but inside the house the fire keeps that part of the stage bright. **Phelim** *is still outside, obviously miserable with the cold, but inside* **Stewart** *sits at his table with the authority of the master of the house, finishing what has plainly been a fully satisfactory repast. He alone of the company is happy and at ease; he sits in an armchair which has been unused during the first two acts.* **Cantwell** *sits by the door, and* **Sally** *stands over him with her hatchet in her hand. On the further side of the room* **Mrs. Moodie** *watches him grimly, a large pistol pointed across her forearm in his general direction.* **Mrs. Stewart** *waits upon her husband, her face marked by anxiety; in this act, for the first time, she wears her cap;* **Mrs. Traill** *sits bolt upright in a chair, glaring at* **Cantwell** *and knitting in an ominous manner.)*

Stewart: This is delicious! The food in York was really abominable. I know of nowhere that I can eat so well as in my own home. Another slice of meat, I think, my dear. And will you be so good as to refill this tankard? Beer is a great comfort — a very great comfort. All I could get in York was rebellion whisky. Made last week I believe it was, too. Imagine if you can, a very inferior quality of gin, hideously sophisticated with molasses and with a strong hint of untanned hides about it, and you have the flavour of rebellion whisky.

*(**Mrs. Stewart** replenishes his tankard in silence.)*

I had some hope that the Archdeacon might have asked me to take a bottle of claret with him, but he had locked his wine-cellar and buried the key until the trouble was over. A Low Church action if ever I heard of one. The Governor, of course, had fled to Niagara in order, I suppose, to get a clearer perspective of the fighting in York. The justices and all the more reputable lawyers were drilling with borrowed weapons on the lawn at Osgoode, and were so delighted to be soldiers, and so eager to plague poor Fitzgibbon with their notions of strategy that there was no diverting them. So you see there wasn't a house where I could get a Christian bite or a cup of drinkable drink. Even the York ladies have forsworn tea, though their houses are full of it. Why do people become so damnably self-denying in wartime? They have decent victual; what's to be gained by not eating properly? It was the same with the rebels. "We've no time to eat," they'd cry; "we must snatch a crust on the run!" And the result was that they ate enormously, at all the wrong times, to keep their strength up.

Mrs. Stewart: Thomas! You didn't mingle with the rebels?

Stewart: Let us say that the rebels mingled with me. Quite a number of them took me for one of themselves because I had no uniform and no gun.

Mrs. Stewart: No gun!

Stewart: Oh, I had my pistols, but I left them at the inn.

Mrs. Traill: It appears to me that this rebellion is being conducted in an uncommonly slipshod fashion.

Stewart: You are quite right, ma'am. I had never realized before what necessities uniforms are in a battle. Without them, how can a man decide whom he should kill? The loyalists looked such ruffians, and the rebels looked so mild that you couldn't tell which from t'other. I should think that perhaps a third of the men in York were fighting on the wrong side and didn't know it.

Mrs. Moodie: You make light of a grave matter, sir.

Stewart: I am aware of it. But pray remember that I have seen this rebellion and you have not.

Mrs. Traill: Was there no bloodshed?

Stewart: There was a battle one evening. The loyalists marched north, and the rebels marched south, and when they met there was a battle of a kind. I'd describe it as a skirmish if it were not the only battle I've ever seen, but I don't pretend to be a judge. A handful of poor fellows were killed, and a few more were wounded, and then the rebels broke and ran. Mackenzie got away, and I suppose he will make for the States. A good many prisoners were taken and there will be some hangings; the school-children are being given a holiday to see them. It's a form of practical education which I can't say I like, but the professional educators must be allowed to know best, I suppose. You may take it from me, the back of the rebellion is broken.

Mrs. Moodie: You mean that it is all over?

Stewart: By no means. The bitterest part has just begun. But there will be no more fighting. What now remains is to hound down and punish anyone who can be associated with the insurrection. That will provide some of our people with agreeable work for a year or more.

Mrs. Moodie: Mr. Stewart, you speak very strangely. It might almost be supposed that you sympathize with the rebels.

Stewart: I bear a humble part in the government of this colony, ma'am. I do not sympathize with any armed outbreak against law and order. But a grave suspicion assails me that what we have at York is order without law. And that is tyranny, Mrs. Moodie.

Mrs. Moodie: A new country needs strong government.

Stewart: The fashion of government is changing everywhere in the world, and has been doing so since the revolution in France. This little upheaval at York is a part of that change.

Mrs. Moodie: It is Methodism which is at the root of it. Religious disunity is the trouble.

Stewart: One can pay too dear for unity of any kind. I don't really think that rebellion is such a very bad thing.

Mrs. Stewart: Thomas!

Mrs. Moodie: Have you no desire for order, sir? For peace?

Stewart: There was once a rebellion in Heaven, you know — the one which sent the Devil to exercise his talents upon Earth. I have often wondered if that was the last of Heaven's troubles.

Mrs. Moodie: You are in a strange mood, sir.

Stewart: I have been compelled to question a system of which I form a part. Luckily most of my colleagues have avoided this discomfort.

Mrs. Traill: May we expect our husbands home soon, do you know?

Stewart: Set your mind at rest; the military will be needed for many months, and perhaps for a year or more. I do not know whether this is good or ill news, but Lieutenant Moodie and Lieutenant Traill are shortly to go to Niagara, to command troops there, and to remain in the service as long as they are wanted. They will be on full pay, of course.

Cantwell: That will be good news, indeed.

Sally: Hush, bad man!

Cantwell: Mrs. Moodie, would you be good enough to direct that pistol at the ceiling. In the stress of your emotion you might discharge it.

Mrs. Moodie: Be silent, sir, until the Honourable Mr. Stewart is ready to address you. As for this pistol, let me inform you that I can shoot a squirrel from a branch at fifty yards.

(She twirls the pistol adroitly upon her finger.)

Mrs. Stewart: The news from York, then, is very good.

Stewart: Yes, when we think what it might have been. Not all good though. Grimaldi is dead.

(He has spoken seriously for the first time. Pause.)

I see that none of you thinks very much of that. But I do. Poor old Joey! Here in the backwoods we yearn for many of the things of home, and will you believe that I have yearned for a sight of Joe Grimaldi as often as anything?

Mrs. Traill: A clown, Mr. Stewart?

Stewart: Yes, a clown. A prince of clowns. There was a great spirit in Joey. Many a time I have laughed at him until I hurt all over. He died last May, and I heard nothing about it until I went to York to do my duty in the rebellion of Upper Canada. Did you ever see him?

Mrs. Moodie: Never.

Mrs. Traill: Papa did not consider the theatre to be wholly serious.

Stewart: And you never saw him, I think, my dear?

Mrs. Stewart: No.

Stewart: He had such a very droll way of saying the simplest things. But I mustn't run on about him. You never saw him, and you don't know what the world has lost.

Cantwell: I saw him many times, Mr. Stewart.

Stewart: You did?

Cantwell: And I grieve with you at his loss.

Stewart: Yes, it really is a loss isn't it? So much more than if it had been some dull, worthy fellow that one knew quite well.

Mrs. Moodie: Mr. Stewart, I warn you that you will be made a fool of! It is this man's habit to find everybody's weak spot and work upon it. Don't let him abuse your interest in this wretched clown!

Stewart: Your pardon, ma'am, but he wasn't a wretched clown. *(Thumping the table.)* He was the greatest clown of our day, or of any day, if you ask me. You've heard Joey sing "Hot Codlings," of course?

Cantwell: A score of times.

Stewart: When I was at Trinity I used to do an imitation — not very good of course —

(He borrows his wife's cap, puts it on, and makes a Grimaldi grin — eyes flashing, and tongue lolling out like a dog's. As he sings the song he drums with knife and fork upon his plate, tankard and the table itself. **Mrs. Stewart** *smiles as though accustomed to such behaviour but the* **Strickland** *sisters do not know what to make of it.)*

Stewart: A little old woman her living she got
By selling hot codlings, hot, hot, hot;
And this little old woman, who codlings sold,
Tho' her codlings were hot she felt herself cold.
So to keep herself warm, she thought it no sin
To fetch for herself a quartem of —

Cantwell: *(Shouts, very loudly.)* *"GIN!"*

Stewart: Oh, for shame!

Both: Ri tol iddy iddy, ri tol lay.

(Phelim hears the singing in the house and creeps to the door during the second verse. This time Stewart uses a plate as a tambourine, beating it on his elbows, head, knees, and, at the culminating line, on his fundament.)

Stewart: This little old woman, while muzzy she got,
       Some boys stole her codlings, hot, hot, hot;
       Powder under her pan put and in it round stones
       Says the little old woman, "These apples have bones!"
       The powder the pan in her face did send
       Which sent the old woman on her latter —

Cantwell and Phelim: *"END!"*

Stewart: Oh, you naughty man!

All Three: Ri tol iddy iddy, ri tol lay.

(During this verse Cantwell has accompanied Stewart by whistling and clapping his hands. At the chorus Phelim, still outside, dances a lively jig and twirls his stick.)

Cantwell: You are an excellent mimic, sir. You bring Joey to life as well as anyone I have ever seen.

Stewart: Thank you; you flatter me.

Mrs. Moodie: He does, and he'll disarm you with flattery.

Stewart: I think not. But did I not hear another voice in the chorus? Was that you, Phelim?

Phelim: *(without)* It was, Your Honour, and it's a fine, strong, manly voice ye have, and you sittin' snug and easy by your fireside.

Stewart: You see, Phelim wants to disarm me by flattery, too. But I have been a magistrate too long not to be able to swallow flattery in gobs without allowing it to affect my decision in the least. As I shall demonstrate now. My dear, will you remove my plate? It detracts from the perfect dignity of the law.

(Smiling, she removes her cap from his head, as well.)

Thank you. Mr. Cantwell, I am now ready to question you.

Cantwell: Before you do so, sir, may I ask what right you have to question me, and by what right you hold me here at — if I judge Sally's intentions correctly — the peril of my life?

Stewart: I shall give you an honest answer. I hold you here because I've got you here and you can't get away. It is a rather novel form of *habeas corpus*. Possession is nine points of the law, and I've got you.

Cantwell: You are very frank. But I take it that you don't mean to kill me.

Stewart: I am only a magistrate. If I kill you it must be inadvertently.

Cantwell: When I get away, then, what will you do if I complain to the proper authority that I have been held against my will?

Stewart: As I am the proper authority to whom such a complaint should be addressed I shall tell you to go to the Devil.

Cantwell: There are higher authorities elsewhere.

Stewart: And I shall tell them that I held you for questioning because I suspected you of sympathy with the rebels.

Cantwell: I shall make a counter-accusation that you yourself sympathize with the rebels.

Stewart: Nobody will believe you. Justice is not a perfect instrument, Mr. Cantwell, and you had better recognize that in this affair I am on the right side and you are on the wrong side. I have you, sir, over a barrel.

(He beckons, and **Cantwell** *moves to a chair across the table from him.)*

Cantwell: Very well, sir. What is the charge against me?

Stewart: I have not the slightest idea. But your accusers are at hand. Ladies, do you wish to make a joint accusation against this person, or shall I consider your grievances individually?

(**Phelim,** *who has been harkening at the door, bursts excitedly into the room.*)

Phelim: Lemme speak, your honour! Sure, and can't I tell the tale agin' the whole lot of 'em! Wasn't they sneakin' and whisperin' with himself when you were from home defendin' us all agin' the bloody rebels?

Stewart: Phelim, get out!

Phelim: Yez have got to hear me evidence! I'm the main witness to the whole disgraceful affair.

Stewart: Be off! I'll deal with you presently.

Phelim: Ain't I a sufferer from him? Didn't he stay here the whole day to keep me from me lawful child and me nearly lawful wife?

Stewart: If there is one thing I cannot abide in a court it is lack of discipline! Sally, give me the poker. Now do you see this, Phelim? This is the mace of this court. I lay it here on the table before me. So long as the mace is in its position the court must be obeyed without question. If you raise your voice again I'll remove the mace from its place of honour and give you a good skelping with it. Now — sergeant-at-arms! Sally, I mean you! Remove the man Phelim Brady; he has no place here; he has merely come inside to get warm! Phelim, wait in the witness room until I call you.

Phelim: Sure and where's the witness room, your honour?

Stewart: It is all of Upper Canada except this chamber, Phelim. Out you go!

(**Sally** *hastens* **Phelim** *out into the cold; as soon as the door is closed he creeps back to listen.*)

Stewart: Phelim has hinted at misconduct of a particular kind in which you ladies and Mr. Cantwell were involved. I may say at once that I regard any such accusations as too ridiculous to be entertained.

Cantwell: Of course such a notion is ludicrous!

Stewart: Mr. Cantwell, one of these ladies is my wife, and so far as I am concerned, above suspicion. On behalf of Mrs. Moodie and Mrs. Traill, I repeat that such a notion is ridiculous, but you show very little feeling for words when you suggest that it is ludicrous.

Cantwell: Your gallantry, sir, is obviously greater than my own.

Stewart: Very likely.

Mrs. Traill: I resent this masculine exchange, which I feel to be derogatory to myself and my sister. It is not by our beauty or our attractiveness to your sex that we seek to justify our existence.

Mrs. Moodie: And it was not through these agencies that Mr. Cantwell sought to offend us.

Stewart: Then pray how did he offend you?

Mrs. Traill: Do you suppose, sir, that a woman has no feelings save those of female vanity?

Stewart: No, madam, I do not suppose anything so stupid, and I must ask you not to fly at me when I am trying to help you.

Mrs. Traill: I have not flown at you, as you put it.

Stewart: Come now, Catherine, don't be vexed. What has he done?

Mrs. Traill: It is by no means easy to say precisely what he has done.

Stewart: Was he rude to you?

Mrs. Traill: No, nothing so trivial.

Mrs. Moodie: We are not children, Mr. Stewart, to take offence at trifles.

Stewart: Did he employ any violence — any physical force?

Cantwell: Do I look like a brigand, sir?

Stewart: If I ask if it is a case of offensive language I am rebuked by the plaintiffs. If I suggest that it was physical assault I am sneered at by the defendant. The position of a judge under such circumstances is an impossible one. Frances, will you be good enough to tell me what is the matter? Why did you all insist when I came home that I do something desperate to Mr. Cantwell at once?

Mrs. Stewart: I suppose that we were overwrought, Thomas.

Stewart: Well? What put you in such a state?

Mrs. Stewart: It was his horrible words about what had gone on this afternoon.

Stewart: He said that he had tempted you all. Was that it?

Mrs. Stewart: Yes.

Stewart: That remark, and the violent exception which you ladies took to it, persuaded me to put Mr. Cantwell under this rather crude form of arrest. Why can you not tell me what he has done?

Mrs. Stewart: Thomas, dear, you have created an atmosphere in which that is very difficult.

Stewart: I am sorry for that, Frances, but it is the only atmosphere I knew for an enquiry.

Mrs. Stewart: But you treat the whole thing as an elaborate joke.

Stewart: Well — consider, my dear. This fellow says that he has tempted you, and Mrs. Moodie and Mrs. Trail — all in an afternoon. I know you all three far too well to attach the obvious meaning to his words. And if he didn't mean the obvious thing, what serious meaning can they have? Shall I ask Cantwell himself to explain what he has done?

Mrs. Stewart: No, Thomas, pray don't do anything of the kind.

Mrs. Traill: No, that would certainly be most undesirable.

Mrs. Moodie: He would merely make worse a situation which is already bad enough.

Stewart: But why is it bad? Will no one tell me?

Mrs. Moodie: Yes, Mr. Stewart. I shall tell you. He has made fools of us. That may not sound impressive. I assure you that it feels very painful.

Stewart: Made fools of you? How?

Mrs. Moodie: Perhaps I should speak only for myself. Mr. Cantwell, by playing upon a foolish side of my nature, led me to feel emotions, and to admit ambitions, to which I had no right.

Stewart: And am I to know more? I mean, were these emotions and ambitions of a very private nature?

Mrs. Moodie: Yes.

Mrs. Traill: You understand, Mr. Stewart, that in every heart there are desires which can never be fulfilled, and which are cherished all the more closely for that reason. Many worldly people think that only carnal desires are nourished and grieved over in that way. But some of us know that intellectual passion can hurt as terribly as any flame of love. People laugh at intellectual women, as cruel people laugh at ugly women, and mock their yearnings and disappointments. But a devoted and loving wife may know an agony of frustration which has nothing at all to do with her marriage; it is the frustration of the mind.

Stewart: I begin to see what has been happening here. It is something far beyond the jurisdiction of this enquiry or of any court I have ever heard of. What a scoundrel you are, Cantwell!

Cantwell: Am I? You are delivering an emotional judgement upon a supposed emotional injury which these ladies think that I have done them. How do you know that, if you were not in such high spirits about the failure of the rebellion in York, you might not dismiss the whole thing as a foolish female vapour?

Stewart: I have no wish to split hairs. I don't intend to pry into things which are unanswerable.

Cantwell: But I delight in splitting hairs, and unanswerable problems are the only ones which can hold my attention for two minutes. You have called me a scoundrel without hearing my side of the case. What sort of a judge do you call yourself?

Stewart: I am not upon trial, sir.

Cantwell: These ladies will tell you that I have not laid a hand upon them, nor have I said a word to them which they bade me unsay. Mr. Magistrate, you find yourself presiding over a court which is faced by a moral issue, and I suggest that you drop your jocular manner and sharpen your wits.

Stewart: How dare you speak to me like that?

Cantwell: The ladies will tell you that I dare to say what other men fear to say.

Phelim: *(outside)* Watch him now, your honour! Mind, or he'll have you destroyed!

Sally: *(Opening the door and speaking directly into* **Phelim**'s *face.)* Quiet!

Mrs. Moodie: I think that Mr. Cantwell has shown the matter in its true light. His offence was a moral one, and not capable of judgement here or perhaps anywhere. Let us drop the matter.

Stewart: Good God, madam, are you his accuser or his lawyer?

Mrs. Moodie: Any offence which Mr. Cantwell gave me was made possible by my own foolishness and vanity. I am as much to blame as he.

Mrs. Traill: I think that I may say the same. Perhaps we should go home now.

Stewart: Frances, will you tell me what has been going on? I am utterly flabbergasted by the whole business.

Mrs. Stewart: I think that Catherine and Susanna are too noble, too self-accusing. I have no wish to pursue any enmity against Mr. Cantwell myself. I think, however, that they should at least have an apology.

Stewart: I am not an inquisitive man. I hear enough of other people's troubles without inviting confession. But I return to my home. A man greets me with the news that he has successfully tempted my wife and her two closest friends. I cannot get one crumb of undisputed, factual information as to what he has done. Everybody accuses everybody else — including me — and now two of the complainants have decided to accuse themselves. This business has driven me to a pitch of curiosity which I cannot sustain much longer without internal combustion.

Cantwell: The ladies feel that you lack the subtlety of intellect to understand their difficulty.

Stewart: I resent that suggestion; I am as subtle as is good for anybody to be.

Cantwell: You will not be contented with an apology, then?

Stewart: No. There is nothing I despise so much as an apology.

Cantwell: *(rising)* That's as well, for I have no intention of apologizing. I have done nothing which appears to me to call for retraction on my part. I tempted these ladies; I did so intentionally; I succeeded and I am satisfied. How long have I been your neighbour, Mr. Stewart?

Stewart: I don't know.

Cantwell: You are the great man in these parts. Wasn't it your business to know?

Stewart: Your settlement papers were in order. That was all that concerned me.

Cantwell: Was it nothing that I was a man of your own class, a countryman of yours? Are Irish gentlemen so common here that you feel no curiosity about them?

Stewart: If you are complaining that I did not make a social call upon you I assure you that I am too busy for such formalities.

Cantwell: And Mrs. Stewart was too busy to call upon Mrs. Cantwell?

Stewart: My wife uses her own discretion in such matters.

Cantwell: And it would have been indiscreet to call upon Mrs. Cantwell because rumours about her had reached you from Ireland?

Mrs. Stewart: That is unjust, sir.

Cantwell: No, not unjust; merely a statement of disagreeable fact. You put a slight upon me and my wife.

Stewart: *(uncomfortably)* In time we would have made your acquaintance. Don't exaggerate, man.

Cantwell: Perhaps you do not realize what a tight, snug, unapproachable little society you have here in Upper Canada. I am not surprised that you have brought a rebellion upon yourselves.

Mrs. Moodie: Do you mean that you did what you did in revenge upon us?

Cantwell: Do you recall your boast to me, this morning, that there was no temptation in the forest? It was you, Mrs. Traill, who said that there was nothing here which might lead ladies of gentle birth and good education astray. You were mistaken.

Stewart: *(Rising, takes the poker back to the fire.)* How were you led astray? You can't have let this man pop some wicked idea into your heads.

Mrs. Moodie: Yes. That is exactly what we did do.

Stewart: Well, God bless my soul! But surely that's simple enough. Pop the idea out again.

Cantwell: Let them do so if they can.

Stewart: You have a great opinion of yourself as a tempter, haven't you?

Cantwell: Yes.

Phelim: *(outside)* He's the Devil, I'm tellin' yez. Why haven't yez got the sense to hear what I'm saying?

Stewart: I wish Phelim would stop shouting that you are the Devil. We don't have the Devil in the nineteenth century, and we certainly don't have him in this country.

Cantwell: These ladies have nothing to worry about then. Now may I go?

Stewart: I can see no reason for detaining you, though I do wish that somebody would tell me what the idea was that caused so much commotion.

Cantwell: Now that you have virtually acquitted me of injuring these ladies, I shall be happy to tell you myself. I have observed that there is one temptation which only the strongest spirits can resist. It is the temptation of discontent.

Stewart: Discontent?

Cantwell: Yes. It is only the crude seducer who takes a woman's honour, and in order to do that he must have some liking for her. It is a more lasting and serious injury to rob her of her peace of mind. These ladies will never, I think, know perfect content again. They will say to themselves that my temptation was beneath contempt, but they will never be free from it. It will always linger at the heart's core. And yet a little humility this morning, and a little charity towards Mrs. Cantwell a few months ago, might have spared them this distress.

Mrs. Moodie: Who are you, to cast our sins of omission in our teeth, and to stand in judgement upon us?

Cantwell: That, Mrs. Moodie, is a matter which I prefer to leave in doubt.

Mrs. Moodie: And all that you have said — you whose opinion Byron valued — was flattery? No grain of truth in it?

Cantwell: That also I prefer to leave in doubt.

Mrs. Moodie: If it gives you satisfaction, sir, that doubt will gnaw at me all my life.

Cantwell: That is as I intend it, madam. You have no further need of me, I believe? Then permit me to make my adieux.

(He bows to Mrs. Moodie *and* Mrs. Traill *in turn, and good breeding demands that they curtsy; he crosses to* Mrs. Stewart *who stands by the door, ready to hand him his cap.)*

Mrs. Stewart, I shall not forget your message.

*(He says this just loud enough for **Stewart** to hear, and as she curtsies he gives **Stewart** a look of triumph. He goes into the yard, and there eyes **Phelim**, who backs away from him in fear.)*

Phelim, you are ninety different kinds of a scoundrel, but I think you have the best pair of eyes in these parts. Drink my health at your wedding.

*(He throws him a coin, and goes, humming his Irish jig. **Phelim** rushes into the house.)*

Phelim: He's gone! Are yez all unharmed?

Stewart: Perfectly unharmed, Brady — I think.

Phelim: Then plase, your honour, can I have me justice now? It's bitter cold outside.

Stewart: Very well. Justice hot and strong for you, Phelim. Sally, tell the girl to come in.

*(**Sally** admits **Honour** from the kitchen. She has the child in her arms.)*

Stewart: Now, Honour, do you want to marry this old rascal?

Honour: I promised his late wife I'd do so, and I'm a woman of my word.

Mrs. Stewart: But, Thomas, the girl cannot go to Phelim's cabin so long as you-know-what is on the roof.

Stewart: I quite agree, my dear. But you-know-what is no longer there. I passed your cabin on my way home, Phelim, and I ordered Barney Flynn to bury your late wife at once. Now you get away before nightfall to Father Clary and make your peace with him as best you may, for I will not have any more of your unchristian antics in the range of my jurisdiction. And if Father Clary permits — and I have my reasons for thinking he will — you and Honour can be married in three days. Meanwhile she is to remain here. Now, Honour, I want you to keep this man in order, and if he lets a rebellious thought out of him, you are to tell me at once.

Phelim: Yez'll permit me just one harmless kiss, your honour, from the girl that's to be me bride?

Honour: Yez have had all the kisses ye'll get from me, Phelim, for a good year and maybe more. Get away to Father Clary at once, as his honour says.

Phelim: Look at her, would yez — as conceited as if she'd cut a dead dog in two with a dull knife! Ah, wasn't I the big fool to take his coin! And sure I'll be in the Devil's own hand from this day!

(He goes, and is seen to wander disconsolately off into the forest. **Honour** *goes to the kitchen with her child.)*

Stewart: Well, does that tie up everything with a bit of blue tape?

Mrs. Stewart: You have done very well, my dear.

*(***Sally*** *puts two lighted candles upon the table, for it is now winter dusk outside.)*

Mrs. Traill: We too should go if we are not to be very late in getting home.

Stewart: Quite out of the question. Anyhow, you haven't heard half my news. Susanna, I hear that Moodie is to have a government post.

Mrs. Moodie: You couldn't possibly be — mistaken?

Stewart: No. It's quite certain. It will mean giving up his farm.

Mrs. Moodie: Giving up his farm? Giving up this backwoods life? Giving up uncertainty, and poverty and debt? Oh, God! *(She bursts into tears.)*

Mrs. Stewart: Catherine, will you take her into the back bedroom. It shall be yours tonight. You need rest, my dear. Later we shall have supper.

(She gives **Mrs. Traill** *one of the candles.)*

Mrs. Traill: Come along, my dear. You must try to compose yourself. We mustn't give way before the servants.

(They go through the door to the kitchen quarters.)

Stewart: If I had known that she would take it so hardly I should have told her later, when fresh tea was made.

Mrs. Stewart: I am sure that there is no harm done. It has come as a great relief.

Stewart: They'll be set up for life, now. I suppose the thought of getting away from that wretched farm, combined with today's trouble, and the thought of the rebellion and all, has discomposed her.

Mrs. Stewart: *(Fetching a chair to the fire for him, and placing a footstool for his lame foot.)* Catherine and Susanna were not too much concerned about the rebellion. Not about their husbands, I mean. They know what soldiering is, I don't. I am so happy to see you safely back, Thomas.

Stewart: *(Goes to her, and sits in the chair.)* Thank you, my dear.

Mrs. Stewart: Would you like to have your slippers?

Stewart: You don't think that Susanna and Catherine would consider it a trifle offhand if I wore them?

Mrs. Stewart: Oh I'm sure they wouldn't.

Stewart: Then I should like them more than anything.

(**Mrs. Stewart** *brings them from under the bunk, right. She kneels at his feet and draws off his boots. He winces as she draws off the boot from the lame leg.)*

Mrs. Stewart: Would you like me to rub your leg, Thomas?

Stewart: Thank you. *(She does so.)* That helps. It is very kind of you to do this.

Mrs. Stewart: Is it particularly kind today? I have done it often.

Stewart: Yes; particularly kind today. I am never unconscious, my dear, that as a husband I lack something in beauty, and agility.

Mrs. Stewart: Oh Thomas, what nonsense!

Stewart: You could have done better. Don't think I don't know it.

Mrs. Stewart: When you fish for compliments, Thomas, you should take more care to hide your hook.

Stewart: Ah, I see that you have been spoiled for my conversation by the polished style of Mr. Cantwell.

Mrs. Stewart: That detestable man!

Stewart: An insinuating fellow, all the same. Anyone who could find a chink in the armour of Susanna and Catherine is no fool.

Mrs. Stewart: Do you mean that a fool could find the chink in mine, Thomas?

Stewart: No, my dear, I do not mean that. Was it very painful?

Mrs. Stewart: It was — unexpected.

Stewart: I had always expected that some day someone would appear who would talk to you about Rossmore.

Mrs. Stewart: Then you guessed what my temptation was?

Stewart: I believe that many husbands think from time to time of the men their wives might have married. *(Pause.)* The message of which Cantwell spoke was for Rossmore, I suppose?

Mrs. Stewart: Oh Thomas, after so many years, are you jealous?

Stewart: No, but I am not complacent, either. I have never taken you for granted, Frances. I do not suppose that a day passes that I do not thank God for the blessing of our life together.

Mrs. Stewart: You make me feel very humble, Thomas.

Stewart: I did not intend to do so; I thought I was the one who should be humble.

Mrs. Stewart: But today — when that man put discontent into my heart — I should have thought of you.

Stewart: Is there a man anywhere who is capable of filling the whole of a woman's heart forever? I know that such fellows exist in romances, but I doubt their reality. *(Pause.)* If I may ask — you needn't answer — is Rossmore that sort of man?

Mrs. Stewart: How can I possibly know? It is many years since I last saw him, and when I think of him now, which is rarely, I think of him as he was then, and I see him, sometimes, with the eyes of a girl. But if we were to meet again I am sure that the whole thing would dissolve. That was where Cantwell was so clever, and so cruel; from something which was past he created, only for a few moments, something which had never been. What he roused in me was not regret, but discontentment, disguised as regret.

Stewart: Hoping, I suppose, that it would work like slow poison.

Mrs. Stewart: But he had reckoned without you.

Stewart: He had reckoned without *us*.

(She is now sitting on the floor beside his chair and they are both looking into the fire. A happy pause.)

Mrs. Stewart: I should be getting tea, and calling Susanna and Catherine.

Stewart: Do not be hasty, my dear. Let us enjoy our victory a little longer.

(During the last scene it has become much darker outside and the first flakes of snow have begun to fall.)

(Curtain)

Notes

Notes are not given in explanation of words that may be found in a large dictionary.

Page 15   Maria Edgeworth: English novelist (1767-1849), celebrated for her tales of mystery and her novels of Irish life.

Page 17   "cottage loaf": a round loaf of three layers — a broad base, smaller second storey, and a nubbin on top.
"poke bonnets": a bonnet with a projecting rim. There are examples in many museums of pioneer life.

Page 18   "caps under their bonnets": Victorian married women wore caps except when in full evening dress; unmarried women and girls did not do so. For a probable explanation see I Corinthians, chapter 11, vv. 1-15.

Page 21   "Mackenzie": William Lyon Mackenzie (1795-1861), leader of the Rebellion to seek redress against Sir Francis Bond Head and the Family Compact. Mackenzie had been elected first mayor of Toronto in 1834, so his attempt to take charge of the city in 1837 was perhaps not so rebellious as it is sometimes represented. His grandson, William Lyon Mackenzie King (1874-1950), was a controversial Canadian statesman, and five times Prime Minister.
"Susanna's 'Oath'": to be found in Chapter 17 of Mrs. Moodie's celebrated *Roughing It in the Bush*.

Page 24   "curtsies": these were not deep curtsies, to the ground, but were performed by putting one foot behind the other, and bending the knees, inclining the head forward but not bending the back. A well-considered curtsy could convey dignity, coquettishness, chilly contempt — an endless variety of comments upon the person curtsied to.

Page 28   "shape its head": this was often done, with great success and no harm to the child, during the first three months

Page 29   "Galway whiskers": a short beard framing the face, but leaving the chin, upper lip and mouth uncovered.
"shebeener": a shebeen is the lowest sort of Irish tavern.

Page 30   "ye": should not be too carefully pronounced, so that it sounds more like "yuh."
In this play variations of accent and niceties of pronunciation are important. Mrs. Stewart speaks with an

educated Irish accent, and there is perhaps no purer or more beautiful form of English speech; Mrs. Moodie and Mrs. Traill are English ladies, so that their speech is not so soft as Mrs. Stewart's but is of great clarity and precision; Phelim and Honour have Irish peasant accents, which are also beautiful in their way, but some of their pronunciations — "crature" for "creature," to specify one — are reminders of the eighteenth century. Cantwell, like Mrs. Stewart, charms with his Irish speech; however he uses it to assist him in his wickedness. This play is written to be heard, as well as seen.

Page 35   Byronic-Satanic: the reputation of George Gordon Noel, Baron Byron of Rochdale (1788-1824) for wickedness was greatly enhanced by his extraordinary personal beauty; he was said to have looked like a Fallen Angel. Many men of his time and in the years immediately following his death, imitated his careless arrangement of his hair, his open shirt-collar, and his air of romantic displeasure.

"wamus": a beaded leather shirt, often of buck or doeskin, usually caught in at the waist with a decorative sash.

Page 38   "cholera morbus": the disease which killed so many of the early settlers was in fact Asiatic cholera, but many of them called it cholera morbus, pleased, perhaps, by the important Latin sound.

Page 39   "case-bottle": a bottle with a protective leather outside.

Page 42   "a goat fly out of his chimney": the Devil frequently appeared to his human devotees in the form of a goat, and in this form he was worshipped at meetings of witches.

Page 46   "Ultima Thule": the farthest north, the jumping-off place. Mrs. Moodie's use of this classical phrase is an evidence of an education which was, in her time, more usual among men than women.

Page 48   "How wise ye are!": Phelim has also used this expression on page 35. It is, of course, ironic.

Page 50   Cantwell's description of the hunting scene is in the romantic manner of the novelist Charles Lever. Irish fox-hunting was notoriously daring and exciting and accidents were frequent.

Page 54   "what Gilbert White did for Selborne": Gilbert White (1720-93) was an English clergyman, famous for his *Natural History and Antiquities of Selborne*, in Hampshire, which was published in 1789; the book is distinguished not only for its knowledge but also for the charm of its writing.

Page 59   "I was a friend of Byron": see note to page 35. The reputation of Byron was still great in literary circles at this time, and to have known him reveals Cantwell as a man at once aristocratic, of distinguished mind, and a lover of literature — just the sort of critic Mrs. Moodie would not ordinarily meet in the backwoods.

Page 65   "Pegasus at the plough": Pegasus *(accent on the first syllable)* was the winged horse given by Athena to the Muses; at a stroke of his hoof he caused the poetically inspiring fountain of Hippocrene to spring forth on Mount Helicon. During World War II Pegasus, pale blue on a maroon ground, was the insignia of all British airborne troops. There is a story that a peasant once captured Pegasus and hitched him to his plough; when a neighbour commented on the animal's wings his captor replied, "Yes, he'd be a better plough-horse if he were not deformed."

Page 69   "the Archdeacon": this was the great John Strachan (1778-1867) who became first Anglican Bishop of Toronto in 1839; he founded King's College, now the University of Toronto, in 1827, and Trinity College in 1851. In calling him "Low Church" Mr. Stewart may perhaps be making a sly reference to the fact that Strachan was, before he took Anglican orders in 1803, a Presbyterian. The Low Church was evangelical and anti-ritualist in opinion: it should be pointed out that Strachan's foundation, Trinity College, now has the reputation of being a stronghold of the High Church, or sacramental and ritualist party. See his biographies by A. N. Bethune and H. Scadding.

"Osgoode": Osgoode Hall, named for William Osgoode, Chief Justice of Upper Canada from 1792 to 1794, is the home of the Law Society of Upper Canada; built in 1822, it is a fine example of the architecture of the period.

"Fitzgibbon": James Fitzgibbon (1780-1863) was acting adjutant-general of the 2nd West York Regiment, and leader of the Loyalist, or anti-Mackenzie, forces. Knighted in 1850. See his life, *A Veteran of 1812*, by his daughter, M.A. Fitzgibbon.

Page 70   "victual": Mr. Stewart has had a gentleman's education, and knows that this word comes from *victualia*, the neutral plural of *victualis*, which in its turn is from *victus*

— food. But he could just as correctly have said "victuals," as we usually do now.

Page 71   "a humble part in the government": Stewart was a Member of the Legislative Assembly and thus, to some extent, an adherent of the Family Compact.

"rebellion in Heaven": for a fuller account of this exciting upheaval see *Paradise Lost*, published in 1667, by John Milton.

Page 72   "Grimaldi is dead": Joseph Grimaldi (1778-1837) was the greatest of clowns. The most popular comic singer of his day, a great dancer and a remarkable acrobat, he had the rare ability to create laughter by means of the slightest changes of expression, as well as by wild antics. It is because of his supremacy that clowns are called "Joeys" to this day. *Hot Codlings* was the most popular of his songs, and was regularly sung in pantomimes for thirty years after his death. Grimaldi was distinguished by his dynamic energy, and it is this quality that the actor of Mr. Stewart must bring to his imitation.

Page 73   "Trinity": Trinity College, Dublin.

Page 75   "habeas corpus": an Act of 1679, to prevent people from being detained in prison indefinitely, and without proper trial. The words, meaning "Thou shalt have the body. . ." are the opening words of the writ issued under the Act.

"it must be inadvertently": a magistrate has no power to condemn a prisoner to death.

Page 82   "We don't have the Devil . . .": the belief that the Devil is dead, or out of business, is still common, in spite of much evidence to the contrary.

Page 85   "blue tape": tape used to tie up the papers in a law case that was finished. Red tape (actually pink) is still used, and may be purchased from law-stationers, along with sealing-wax, quill pens, and many other things which are often said to be out of existence.

"before the servants": it was a point of good breeding not to give way to emotion, to quarrel, or to contradict anyone when the servants were in the room. Thus arose the expression *pas devant les domestiques*, spoken as a warning to children, as the servants did not usually understand French. The warning *pas devant* is still occasionally heard.

Overlaid

Overlaid

Characters:

Pop

Ethel

George Bailey

First Production: Ottawa Drama League, 1947.

(The scene is a farmhouse kitchen in rural Canada. It is a cluttered and inconvenient room containing a wood range, a dresser, a kitchen table, a radio and several chairs. There is a door leading to the farmyard and another to the house. A light cord, fitted with a double socket, hangs nakedly from the ceiling; a basket of unironed clothes sits under the table; an ironing board and an electric iron are in the corner and on the top of the range respectively.

As the curtain rises the radio rings with the applause of a great audience. **Pop,** *a farmer of seventy, sitting in a kitchen armchair and wearing an ancient and battered top hat, is applauding also; on his hands he wears white cotton workman's gloves.)*

Radio Voice: Once again our principals are led on by Mr. Panizzi . . . and they bow. You can hear the rapturous applause of this Saturday matinee audience. *(Sound of applause rises.)*

Pop: Attaboy! Yippee!

Radio Voice: Our lovely Lucia, in her handsome green and gold first act costume, steps forward to acknowledge a special tribute. . . . *(Tremendous applause.)*

Pop: Hot dog!

Radio Voice: And now, ladies and gentlemen, we have arrived at the first intermission in this Saturday afternoon performance of *Lucia di Lammermoor,* brought to you from the stage of the Metropolitan Opera House in New York City, and in just a few moments I shall ask the president of our Opera Radio Guild, Mrs. August Belmont, to address you.

Pop: Yay, Miz' Belmont!

*(**Ethel,** Pop's daughter, enters; she is a hard-faced woman of forty; she takes the basket of clothes from under the table.)*

Ethel: Poppa, turn that thing down; I can't hear myself think.

Radio Voice *(female)*: Friends of the Opera Guild everywhere. . . .

Pop: Quiet, gal; Miz' Belmont's goin' to speak.

Ethel: I don't care who it is. You always turn it up loudest when they're clapping. My head's splitting.

Pop: Leave 'er be.

Ethel: Oh, don't be so contrary!

(She turns the radio down to a murmur.)

I've got one of my sick headaches; that racket just goes through and through me like a knife. I've got ironing to do out here.

(She sets up her board from the table to a chair back, and then plugs in her iron, climbing on a chair to reach the central light socket.)

Pop: Oh, no, you don't. Bump, bump, bump all through my op'ry. You just wait. Go lie down again. Rest your head.

Ethel: It's got to be done. Can't wait. Plenty to do without waiting till half past five for that row to be over.

Pop: Row, eh? Say, whose house is this anyways? Mine or your'n?

Ethel: Yours, of course, but I do the work and keep things decent and Jim works the farm. You can't expect to have everything your own way; you know that.

Pop: I'll have this my own way. Now you turn up that radio so's I can hear Miz' Belmont.

Ethel: Oh, don't be so childish! What do you want to hear some society woman in New York for?

Pop: What for? Because she's my kind, that's what for! I'm a member of the Op'ry Radio Guild; paid my three bucks and got a ticket says so. This here Miz' Belmont, she's boss of the Guild. Guess I can hear her if I want!

Ethel: Your kind!

(She tests her iron by spitting on it.)

Pop: Yes, my kind and no "ptuh" about it neither. Just because you were a schoolmarm before you married a dumb farmer you think you're everybody, don't you? Well, you never had no ear for music, nor no artistic soul. You ain't never been one of the artistic crowd.

Ethel: And you are, I suppose?

(She is now ironing as though she were punishing the clothes, sprinkling and thumping ill-naturedly.)

Pop: Durn right I am! Look at me! I'm at the op'ry, the only fella in this township that is, I betcha. And where's Jim? Layin' out in the barn asleep, though you think he's workin.' And where are you? Layin' on the bed, hatin' the world and feelin' sick, and he thinks you're workin.' You're emotionally understimulated, the both of you.

Ethel: What did you say?

Pop: You heard me good enough.

Ethel: Listen, Poppa. I've stood a good deal from you, but I won't have that kind of talk.

Pop: What's wrong with it?

Ethel: You know, well enough. Emotion, and that. Suppose little Jimmy was to hear?

Pop: Well, what if he does?

Ethel: A child like that? Putting ideas in his head!

Pop: Do him good. Any ideas he gets in this house he'll have to get from me. You and Jim ain't got none. *(He turns up the radio.)*

Radio voice *(female)*: If our lives lack beauty, we are poor indeed . . .

Ethel: Emotionally understimulated! You were always loose.

Pop: Hey?

Ethel: I know what Mother went through. *(Turns radio down.)*

Pop: Oh, you do, do you? Well, you don't. Your Ma was kinda like you — just as dumb but not as mean.

Ethel: Don't speak so of Mother!

Pop: I knew your Ma better than you did. She worked like a nigger on this farm: we both did. When she wasn't workin' she was up to some religious didoes at the church. Then come forty-five or fifty she broke down and had to have a spell in the bughouse. Never properly got over it. More and more religion: more and more hell-raisin' at home. Folks say I drove her crazy. It's a lie. Emotional undernourishment is what done it, and it'll do the same for you. You an' your sick headaches!

Ethel: Poppa, that's the meanest thing you ever said! You're a wicked old man!

Pop: Yeh, but I'm happy, an' that's more than most of 'em can say 'round here. I'm the Bohemian set of Smith township, all in one man. Now you let Miz' Belmont speak.

(He turns up the radio. **Jimmy***'s voice, the changing voice of a boy of fourteen, is heard outside.)*

Jimmy: Hey, Maw! Hey, Maw!

Radio Voice: No life today need be starved for fulfilment which the noblest art can give. It is to be had for the taking: great music, great drama. . . .

Ethel: *(At the door, fondly.)* What is it, Lover?

Jimmy: Car comin' in from the road.

Ethel: Do you know whose?

Jimmy: Naw; from town by the looks of it.

Ethel: Well, don't get cold, will you, Lover?

(She closes the door and turns down radio.)

Pop: Lover! Huh!

Ethel: Well, what about it? He's my own son, isn't he?

Pop: Yeh. Bet you never called Jim "Lover."

Ethel: Of course not. To a grown person it ain't — isn't decent.

Pop: You said ain't!

Ethel: Living with you it's a wonder any of my Normal School sticks to me at all.

Pop: Never could figure why they call them things Normal. Now who's comin' here to bust in on my Saturday afternoon; the one time o' the week when I get a little food for my immortal soul.

Ethel: *(From window.)* It's that insurance agent from town.

Pop: Aw, him! What's he want?

(A loud knock at the door and **George Bailey** *enters; he is a fat man with a frequent, phlegmy laugh.)*

G. B.: Well, well, lots o' snow you got out here, eh? Afternoon, Miz' Cochran. Hi, Grandpop! Holy Gol, what are you doin' in that get up, for Pete sake?

Pop: Awright now, G. B.; awright; say your say and don't be all day over it. I'm busy.

Ethel: Poppa, what a way to talk to a man who's just come in out of the cold. Will you have a cup of tea, Mr. Bailey?

G. B.: Sure, thanks, if you got it handy.

Ethel: Right on the stove; always keep some going.

G. B.: Now then, Grandpop, what's the big idea? Gettin' ready for an Orange Walk, or something?

Pop: If you got to know, I'm listenin' to the op'ry on the radio. I listen every Saturday afternoon. I'm a paid-up member of the Op'ry Radio Guild, same as Miz' August Belmont. This hat is what is called an op'ry hat, but I guess you wouldn't understand about that.

G. B.: *(uproarious)* Holy smoke! And what's the idea of the furnaceman's gloves?

Pop: In New York white gloves for the op'ry are *dee rigger*. That's French for you can't get in without 'em.

G. B.: *(choking)* Well by gollies, now I seen everything.

Pop: No you ain't: you ain't seen nothin,' nor been anywheres. That's what's wrong with you and a lot more like you. Now what do you want?

G. B.: Keep your shirt on, Grandpop. I'm here on business: 32096B Pay Life is finished, washed up, and complete.

Pop: Hey?

G. B.: Yep. Now, what d'you want to do with the money?

Pop: What money?

G. B.: Your money. Your insurance policy is paid up. You were seventy a couple of days ago, weren't you?

Pop: Yeh.

G. B.: Well, then — you got twelve hundred dollars comin' to you.

Pop: Is that right?

G. B.: You bet it's right. Didn't you know?

Pop: I'd kinda forgotten.

G. B.: Gol, you farmers! I wonder you're not all on relief, the kind of business men you are.

Pop: Aw shut up. I been payin' so long I guess I forgot I was payin' for anything except to save you from honest work. Twelve hundred bucks, eh?

G. B.: A cool twelve hundred.

Pop: When do I get it?

G. B.: Well, now, just a minute, now. You don't have to take the money.

Pop: Oh, I don't, eh?

G. B.: No. There's a couple of options. If you want, we'll give you a hundred dollars a year in twelve equal monthly instalments, for twelve years, and if you die before it's all gone (which you will, o' course) the balance will go to your heirs, minus certain deductions for accounting and adjustment. Or if you'd rather we'll give you two hundred cash and a paid up policy for a thousand, which would give you a smart burial and leave five or six hundred for Miz' Cochran and Jim.

Ethel: Here's your tea.

G. B.: Yeah, thanks. *(Gulps some of it.)* What do you think he ought to do?

Ethel: Well — it's hard to say. With twelve hundred we could make a lot of improvements 'round the farm. I know Jim wants a tractor the worst way. But then, the thousand in the hand after Poppa's called home would certainly be welcome. Of course, we hope that won't be for many years yet.

G. B.: Nope. The old codger looks good for a while yet. Still, you know, Grandpop, at your time of life anything can happen.

Pop: Yeh? Well, with all that fat on you, and that laugh you got, you might have a stroke any minute. Ever look at it that way?

G. B.: By gollies, you're a card. Ain't he a card, eh? Seventy and smart as a steel trap. A regular card.

Pop: You talk like nobody ever lived to seventy before.

G. B.: The average life expectancy for men on farms is sixty-point-two years; you're living on borrowed time, Grandpop.

Pop: Borrowed from who?

G. B.: What a card! Borrowed from who, he says. It's just a way of speaking; technical.

Pop: Borrowed from you, I hope.

G. B.: Aw now, don't get sore. What do you want to do? Personally I'd advise the two-hundred-down-and-a-thousand-at-death plan. Nice, clean cut proposition, and fix up Jim and Miz' Cochran when you're gone.

Pop: I ain't gone yet. I'll take the twelve hundred in cash. Got it on you?

G. B.: Eh? No. I can write you a cheque. But are you sure you want it that way?

Pop: Sure I'm sure.

Ethel: What are you up to, Poppa?

Pop: None of your business.

Ethel: He'll let you know on Monday, Mr. Bailey.

Pop: I just told him. You keep out o' this.

Ethel: Poppa and Jim and I'll talk it over tonight. We'll phone you on Monday.

Pop: You and Jim nothin.' I made up my mind.

Ethel: You haven't considered.

Pop: Say, whose money is this? Ain't it my insurance?

Ethel: Didn't you take it out to provide for your family?

Pop: Damned if I remember what I took it out for after all these years. Likely I took it out because some insurance agent bamboozled me into it. Never knew it would bring me in anything.

Ethel: Now, Poppa, you don't want to do anything foolish after all those years of paying the premium. You took out the policy to protect your family and properly speaking it's family money, and the family will decide what to do with it.

Pop: What makes you so sure I'd do somethin' foolish?

Ethel: Well, what would you do?

Pop: I'd go to New York and spend it — that's what.

Ethel: You'd what?

G. B.: Go on a tear, eh, Grandpop? By gollies, you're a card!

Pop: No, I ain't a card. That's what I'm goin' to do. You can write the cheque right now, and I'll catch the 9:15 into town. I got enough money to get me quite a piece of the ways without cashin' it.

G. B.: Go on! You ain't serious?

Pop: Dum right I'm serious.

G. B.: You can't do that.

Pop: Why not?

G. B.: Because you can't. You don't want to go to New York.

Pop: Who says I don't?

G. B.: You don't know nobody there. Where'd you sleep an' eat?

Pop: Hotel.

G. B.: Go on!

Ethel: He's just keeping this up to torment me, Mr. Bailey.

Pop: You keep out o' this.

G. B.: Lookit, Grandpop — are you serious?

Pop: Say, how often do I have to tell you I'm serious?

G. B.: Aw, but lookit — two hundred'll buy you a nice trip if you got to go somewheres.

Pop: Two hundred won't last a week where I'm goin'! Gimme the twelve hundred an' make it quick!

G. B.: Say lookit — do you know how much twelve hundred dollars is?

Pop: 'Tain't much, but it'll have to do.

G. B.: 'Tain't much! Say lookit, do you know what's wrong with you? You're crazy, that's what! What'd you do in New York with twelve hundred dollars?

Pop: *(Very calmly and with a full sense of the effect of what he says on* **Ethel** *and* **Bailey**.*)* I'll tell you what I'd do, since you're so nosey; I'd get some stylish clothes, and I'd go into one o' these restrunts, and I'd order vittles you never heard of — better'n the burnt truck Ethel calls food — and I'd get a bottle o' wine — cost a dollar, maybe two — and drink it all, and then I'd mosey along to the Metropolitan Opera House and I'd buy me a seat right down beside the trap drummer, and there I'd sit an' listen, and holler and hoot and raise hell whenever I liked the music, an' throw bookies to the gals, an' wink at the chorus, and when it was over I'd go to one o' these here night clubs an' eat some more an' drink whisky, and watch the gals that take off their clothes — every last dud, kinda slow an' devilish till they're bare-naked — an' maybe I'd give one of 'em fifty bucks for her brazeer —

Ethel: *(scandalized)* Poppa!

G. B.: Jeepers!

Ethel: You carnal man!

Pop: An' then I'd step along Park Avenoo, an' I'd go right up to the door, an' I'd say, "Is this where Miz' August Belmont lives?" an' the coon would say, "Yessiree!" an' I'd say, "Tell her one o' the Op'ry Guild gang from up in Canada is here, an' how'd she like to talk over things — "

G. B.: Say listen, Grandpop: you're nuts.

Ethel: He must be. Mother was like that at the last, you know.

Pop: She was not; your Ma used to think the Baptist preacher was chasin' her to cut the buttons off her boots, but that was as far as she got. She never had the gumption to pump up a real good dream. Emotional undernourishment: that was what ailed your Ma.

Ethel: There you go agin! He's been talking that indecent stuff all afternoon.

Pop: 'Tain't indecent. It's the truth. No food for your immortal souls — that's what ails everybody 'round here — little, shriveled-up, peanut size souls. *(He turns up the radio with a jerk.)*

Radio Voice: *(blaring)* . . . render life gracious with the boon of art . . .

Ethel: *(Turning radio down.)* Is that what your soul feeds on? Restrunts with shameless women in 'em?

Pop: Yeah, an' music an' booze an' good food an' high-toned conversation — all the things a man can't get here because everybody's too damn dumb to know they're alive. Why do you think so many people go to the bughouse around here, anyways? Because they've starved an' tormented their souls, that's why! Because they're against God an' don't know it, that's why!

Ethel: That's blasphemous!

Pop: It ain't blasphemous! They try to make God in their own little image an' they can't do it same as you can't catch Niagara Falls in a teacup. God likes music an' naked women an' I'm happy to follow his example.

Ethel: *(Shrieks in outrage.)* Eeeeeek!

G. B.: *(On firm moral ground at last.)* That'll do now! That'll just do o' that! I ain't goin' to listen to no such smut: I got a kiddy at home not three yet! Do you think I'm goin' to give you twelve hundred dollars for that kind o' thing? It wouldn't be business ethics! Say, you better look out I don't report this to the Ministerial Alliance! They'd tell you where you got off, darn soon!

Pop: You mean you won't give me the money?

G. B.: Naw!

Pop: You want me to have to write to head office an' ask why?

G. B.: I'll tell 'em. Unsound mind, that's why.

Pop: What's your proof?

G. B.: You just say what you said about God to any doctor, that's all.

Pop: Yeah, but if I don't?

G. B.: Well —

Pop: You'd look kinda silly, wouldn't you?

G. B.: Now lookit —

Pop: Would it cost you the agency, do you think?

G. B.: Aw, now lookit here —

Pop: A libel suit'd come pretty dear to your company, anyways.

G. B.: Libel?

Pop: Libellous to say a man's crazy.

G. B.: Miz' Cochran would back me up.

Pop: Serious thing, tryin' to put a man in the bughouse just when he gets some money. Look bad in court.

G. B.: *(deflated)* Aw, have it your own way. I'll write you a cheque. He sits at the table and does so.

Pop: Make it nice an' plain, now. *(He turns up the radio.)*

Radio Voice *(male, again)*: You have been listening to Mrs. August Belmont, of the Metropolitan Opera Guild, in one of the series of intermission talks which is a regular feature of this Saturday afternoon broadcast. And now to give you a brief outline of Act II of Gaetano Donizetti's romantic masterwork, *Lucia di Lammermoor*: the curtain rises to disclose the magnificent hall of Sir Henry Ashton's castle. Norman (played this afternoon by the American baritone Elmer Backhouse) tells Sir Henry (Mr. Dudelsack) that he need have no fear that Lucy will offer opposition to the proposed marriage with Lord Arthur Bucklaw (played this afternoon by Listino di Prezzi) as her letters to Edgar (Mr. Posaun in today's performance) have been intercepted and forgeries substituted for them which will leave no doubt of his faithlessness. At this point Lucia (Miss Fognatura) enters (in a gown of greenish blue taffeta relieved by cerise gussets and a fichu) to a delicately orchestrated passage for wind and strings. Then, supported entirely by wind, Lucy tells her brother that her hand is promised to another, whereupon he produces the forged letters. "The papers," she cries: "La lettera, mio dio!" whereupon follows a lively upward rush of brass. . . .

G. B.: *(During the foregoing.)* Here. Well, g' day, Miz' Cochran. *(He listens to the radio ecstasies.)* Cheest! *(He goes out.)*

Ethel: *(Turning the radio down.)* Well?

Pop: Yeh?

Ethel: When you've squandered the money — what then?

Pop: I'll be back. This is my farm, remember. I'll have some stories to tell you, Ethel. Maybe that Home an' School Club o' yours'll ask me to address 'em on my experiences. I'll show 'em the programs from the op'ry — maybe even let 'em see my fifty-buck brazeer. *(A pause.)*

Ethel: *(Sitting down.)* Listen, Poppa; you haven't thought about this.

Pop: Are we goin' to go through all that again?

Ethel: Yes. You know what people will say when you come back. They'll say a fool and his money are soon parted. They'll say there's no fool like an old fool.

Pop: What do I care what they say?

Ethel: This dream of yours is crazy, like Mr. Bailey says. If you go to New York you'll just be a lost old man, and everybody will laugh at you and rob you.

Pop: How do you know?

Ethel: I know. You don't belong there. You belong right here in this township, though you've been ungrateful and abused it, just because it isn't full of opera and restrunts and hussies. This township's been good to you — given you a good living —

Pop: You mean I've been able to work like an ox here and keep the sheriff the other side o' the gate?

Ethel: That's more than many people have had.

Pop: Well 'tain't enough for me. What about my soul? What's this township ever give me for that, eh? There was just one purty thing in sight o' this farm — row of elms along the road; they cut down the elms to widen the road an' then never widened it.

Ethel: You talk about your soul in a way that makes me blush. Soul to you just means the pleasures of the flesh. We got a fine church, with almost half the debt paid off on it —

Pop: Yeah, an' your Ma pretty near bled me white over that debt. Last fifty bucks I gave 'em was for a bell, and what'd they do? Bought a new stove with it.

Ethel: They needed a stove.

Pop: Yeah, an' they needed a bell. But that's always the way around here; necessities first every time.

Ethel: And what's wrong with that?

Pop: Because there's always a gol-danged necessity to get in the way whenever you want somethin' purty. There's always somebody starvin,' or a sewer needs diggin,' or some damn necessary nuisance to hog all your time an' energy an' money if you go lookin' for it. Somebody's got to take the bull by the horns an' ignore the necessities if we're ever goin' to have any o' the things that make life worth livin.'

Ethel: What makes life worth living? You seem to think nothing is worth having but a high old time. Don't you ever think of duty?

Pop: I've had a bellyful o' duty. I've got somethin' in me that wants more than duty an' work.

Ethel: Yes, and you've told me what it is. Rich food and alcohol and lewd women. A fine thing, at your age!

Pop: Aw — that's just a way of speakin.' I want what's warm an' — kind of mysterious; somethin' to make you laugh an' talk big, an' — oh, you wouldn't know. You just sit there, lookin' like a meat axe, an' won't even try to see what I'm drivin' at. Say listen, Ethel, what d'you get out o' life anyways?

Ethel: Well, that's a fine question!

Pop: Now don't get mean about it. You called my New York trip a dream; what's your dream?

Ethel: I'm not the dreaming kind.

Pop: Oh yes you are. You cranky ones, you're the ones with dreams, all right. What do you think o' yourself, Ethel?

Ethel: Well *(pause)* — I think I'm a dutiful woman.

Pop: A good woman?

Ethel: *(Overcoming her aversion to the luxury of direct self-praise.)* Yes.

Pop: And is that what you want out o' life?

Ethel: It's my reward for a lot of work and self-denial.

Pop: Go on.

Ethel: You talk about dreams. Why do you think I live the way I do? Because it's right, first of all. And there are rewards on earth, too. When I walk into church or a meeting I know what people say: they say "There's Ethel Cochran; she stands on her own two feet, and never asks anything from anybody; she has a hard enough row to hoe, too, but you never hear a peep out of her."

Pop: An' you like that, eh? Kind o' strong woman stuff?

Ethel: I'm glad I'm well thought of. "You never see her wash out after Monday noon," they say.

Pop: And that's what you want in life? To be a woman that nobody can help or give anything to? Come on, Ethel; what else?

Ethel: Well — you wouldn't understand.

Pop: I'm trying. Go on.

Ethel: I want to be remembered.

Pop: Yeah? How?

Ethel: You're not going to New York, are you?

Pop: Who says I ain't?

Ethel: Then let's not go on talking.

Pop: Now Ethel, we ain't goin' to stop. I want to know what goes on inside you. Get yourself a cup o' tea, and give me one too an' let's have this out.

*(**Ethel** goes to get the tea.)*

I think I see what you're up to. You don't want me to go to New York because you want that money for somethin' else. Is that it?

Ethel: Here's your tea.

Pop: Sit down.

Ethel: Rather stand.

Pop: Now what is it you want? Not a tractor, I bet. Come on, now. Is it something for Lover? You want to send him to college, maybe?

Ethel: Naturally I want to see Jimmy get a good start in life. I — I've done a little saving toward it.

Pop: Yeah, I know. Cheatin' on me an' Jim. I know where you got it hid, too. But that ain't it. I can tell.

Ethel: Of course you'd make it sound ugly. I'm determined that my boy shall be a pharmacist, and I've had to find my own way of financing it.

Pop: But that ain't your real ambition. Come on, Ethel.

Ethel: No.

Pop: Unless you tell me, I'm certain to go on my trip and spend all the money, and bang goes your dream. But if you tell me, you've got a chance. It's up to you.

(Pours his tea in his saucer and drinks noisily.)

Ethel: That'd look fine in a New York restrunt. What would the brazen women say?

Pop: They'd put up with it long's I had a dollar. Don't stall, Ethel. We got nearest to your dream when you said you wanted to be remembered. Come on, now.

Ethel: I won't tell you.

Pop: Don't, then. *(Rises purposefully.)* Got a clean shirt for me? I'll be getting ready to go.

Ethel: *(Wavers for a moment, then breaks into painful, ugly tears.)* Poppa!

Pop: Yeah?

Ethel: I want — a headstone.

Pop: You want a what?

Ethel: A headstone. A granite one.

Pop: *(Sits, flabbergasted.)* Well, good God Almighty!

Ethel: *(Weeping freely now.)* Mother's grave just has a plain marker. But it's in a wonderful position. Soon all the land around it will be sold off and who can tell where we'll be buried? Higgledy piggledy all over the place, most likely. We ought to have a proper family plot, with a chain fence round it, and a headstone with the family name on it. A headstone! Oh, a big family headstone! We could get that plot surrounding Mother, right on the crest of the hill, and it'd be seen from every place in the cemetery. A headstone! Not a broken pillar, or a draped urn, or anything flashy and cheap, but a great big block of granite — the gray, not the red — smooth finished on the faces, but rough on the sides and top, and the name on the base, cut deep! Dignified! Quiet! But the best quality — the finest in the cemetery. I want it! I want it! Then Mother and I, and Lover and Jim and you could all be there together at last —

Pop: Envied by every stiff in the township!

Ethel: I want it! I want it!

Pop: I can see that.

Ethel: Not even a text. No "Rest in the Lord" or "Till The day Break" or anything. Just the name.

Pop: And that's what you want more than anything else?

Ethel: Yes. You had to know. Now you know. Jim doesn't care about — well, about nice things like that. And of course it isn't his name.

Pop: And when Bailey came in here with twelve hundred bucks for me you seen your gravestone as good as raised?

Ethel: Yes.

Pop: Pretty vain idea, ain't it?

Ethel: No it ain't — isn't. We've been something in this township. You would never run for council, though you could have been reeve if you'd tried. But Mother was a real figure here, especially the four or five years before — she had to go to That Place. And I've tried to follow where she went. She deserves something, and so do I. Missions, Temperance, the W.A. — we've done our share and more. And when we're gone we deserve something that'll last. That money would cover it all, and leave a little something to provide for Perpetual Care. It's not vain to want your due.

Pop: Don't follow your Ma's trail as far as the bughouse, Ethel. It'd cost a darn sight more than my insurance money to keep you there.

Ethel: It was silly of me to tell you. You've got no feeling for anything that really matters. I've just put a stick in your hand to beat me with.

Pop: Drink your tea an' blow your nose an' shut up. Ain't there a pen an' ink someplace here? *He searches in the dresser drawers.* Yeah, here she is. Y'know, I never could play no instrument nor draw worth a cent; but before my fingers got so stiff I was a real pretty writer. Your Ma once got me to write out a presentation address to a preacher that was leavin,' and when it was done it just looked like a page o' copperplate. There, Ethel: there's your cheque, endorsed and made over to you.

(Ethel takes the cheque, amazed.)

Ethel: Poppa!

Pop: Buy yourself a nice tombstone. *(He sits.)* Y'know, when you was a little thing, you was as pretty as all get out, and till you got to be about fourteen you meant more to me than anything else on God's earth. But then you got religion, and began to favour your Ma, and I guess it was as if you'd died to me, and everything I liked. So far as I'm concerned, this here tombstone's mostly for the little one I lost.

Ethel: Poppa, we've had our disagreements, but that's past. It'll be different now.

(She has put the cheque in her pocket, changed her mind, and tucked it in her bosom.)

Pop: Because I bought you a tombstone? Naw. You've changed, Ethel, and you've been what you are more than twice as long as you were my child.

Ethel: But I don't understand. You do this wonderful, generous thing, and yet you seem so bitter. I know you haven't much feeling for me.

Pop: Oh, yes I have; I pity you twelve hundred bucks' worth an' maybe more.

Ethel: But why — ?

Pop: Aw, never mind. Ethel, you've got the power of goodness.

Ethel: *(modest)* Oh, Poppa!

Pop: Don't take it as a compliment. There's a special kind o' power that comes from the belief that you're right. Whether you really are right or not doesn't matter: it's the belief that counts. Your belief in your own goodness makes you awful strong, Ethel, and you've kind of overlaid me with it. I can't stand up to it.

Ethel: I don't know what you're talking about. I don't know what to say about this, Poppa. There must be depths of good in you I never suspected. It just goes to show that we shouldn't judge.

Jimmy's Voice: *(outside)* Hey, Maw!

Pop: There's your future druggist hollerin.'

Ethel: *(At the door, her voice trilling with happiness.)* Yes, Lover?

Jimmy's Voice: How long till supper, Maw?

Ethel: Oh, you greedy thing! More'n an hour. D'you want me to fix you a piece?

Jimmy's Voice: Naw, I'll wait.

Ethel: I'm going to open a jar of maple surrp. Pancakes, Lover! *(She closes the door.)*

Pop: Lover! Emotional understimulation!

(Ethel comes behind him and gives him a dry, shy kiss on the brow. Then she goes to the radio and turns it on, with an indulgent smile toward him. It hums a little as it warms.)

Pop: Naw. Turn it off. Don't want it now. I been overlaid and I got to get myself back in shape. Maybe I been emotionally over-stimulated. But I ain't overlaid for good, Ethel, an' that stone'll rest lighter on me than it will on you.

(During this speech Ethel has been getting flour, bowls and other supplies out of the dresser, with her back to Pop. He has fished a long pair of black stockings out of the clothes basket and wrapped them round his arm like a mourner's crêpe; he now tilts back in his chair and surveys Ethel's back quizzically, whistling an air from Lucia, which mingles with the sound of Ethel's eggbeater as the curtain falls.)

(Curtain)

Notes

Page 97 "*Lucia di Lammermoor*": an Italian tragic grand opera with music by Gaetano Donizetti. It is loosely based on Sir Walter Scott's *The Bride of Lammermoor*.

"Metropolitan Opera House": now, this house is a fourteen-storey opera theatre in the Lincoln Center for the Performing Arts in New York City. It opened in 1966, cost over $42.5 million and seats over 3700 persons. In 1949, when *Overlaid* was first published, the Metropolitan Opera House, although sophisticated for its day, was not as grandiose in size and program as it is today. Pop's desire to sit in on a performance so that he can brag back home that he was part of something grand would be realized more fully if he could sit in the new building. But the old building had great charm.

Page 100 "Bohemian set of Smith Township, all in one man": Pop uses this expression to indicate that he thinks he is the only person in his entire town who lives an unconventional life as an artist.

Page 101 "Normal School": a teacher-training institution, of a type no longer in existence. It was founded on the École Normale in France.

Biography
Robertson Davies, Playwright

Robertson Davies was born on August 28, 1913 in Thamesville, Ontario, the third of three boys. His father was owner and editor of the newspaper, and while the children were growing up he continued to purchase ever-larger papers, including the *Renfrew Mercury*, the Kingston *Whig* (later *Whig-Standard*) and the Peterborough *Examiner*. Both parents enjoyed theatre and often took their three sons to plays with them. Kingston was a particularly good theatre town in the thirties: as well as having three amateur dramatic societies, New York and London travelling productions regularly added Kingston to their Montreal/Toronto itinerary.

For four years Robertson Davies attended Upper Canada College; with his training at home, he naturally fell into editing the school newspaper. "We just thought that writing was something that you did, we never thought of it as a special accomplishment. Just something you had to do like bakers all knowing how to make bread." [1] At UCC Davies also participated in the school's drama club, and continued his active involvement in theatre while attending Queen's University.

As a graduate student at Balliol College, Oxford, Davies again enjoyed working in university productions, as actor, stage manager, and director of the Oxford University Dramatic Society. His 1938 dissertation for his Bachelor of Literature was on Shakespeare's boy actors, and was published the next year by J. M. Dent.

After graduation, Davies acted with an English repertory company for some months before joining London's Old Vic Company. There he acted in minor parts, taught the history of drama at the Drama School, and did editorial work for the director, Tyrone Guthrie.

In 1940 Robertson Davies and Brenda Mathews, a stage manager for the Old Vic, were married. Rejected for military service, Davies returned to Canada, becoming Literary Editor of *Saturday Night* in Toronto. In 1942 he joined the editorial staff of the Peterborough *Examiner*, which was owned by his father, and continued to write articles for *Saturday Night*. The same year his second book, *Shakespeare for Young Players: A Junior Course*, was published, giving advice on choice of scenes, acting and staging.

Selections from his witty weekly newspaper columns, "The Diary of Samuel Marchbanks," were published in two books in 1947 and 1949, giving Davies Canada-wide fame. A further collection, *Samuel Marchbanks' Almanack* was published in 1967.

But theatre was Davies' first love, and he was instrumental in its development in Canada as the country's premier playwright in the important mid-century period. Robertson Davies won the Ottawa Drama League's play writing prize for two consecutive years: in 1947 for *Overlaid*, and the following year for *Eros at Breakfast*. The latter also was awarded the Dominion Drama Award for best production of a Canadian play, and the Gratien Gélinas prize for best playwright. Davies even found time to direct, winning the Louis Jouvet Trophy for his direction of *The Taming of the Shrew* by the Peterborough Little Theatre in 1949; that year he also won the Gélinas prize again, for *Fortune, My Foe*.

Davies wrote his plays to entertain an audience, rather than to proselytize. But it is likely that a favourite Davies theme had an impact on the development of Canadian cultural life, forcing Canadians to consider the importance of the arts in a civilized country.

Over the next years several Canadian companies performed works by Robertson Davies. The Peterborough Little Theatre produced *The Voice of the People* in 1950, and *At My Heart's Core*, a three-act play, was commissioned for the Peterborough Centennial. The Crest Theatre in Toronto, which had been founded with a commitment to Canadian plays, premiered two Davies' plays, *A Jig for the Gypsy* and *Hunting Stuart*. A third play Davies also wrote for the Crest, *General Confession*, was never produced.

Davies played a role in establishing the Stratford Shakespearean Festival, and was elected Governor of the Board of Directors in 1953. Davies worked to ensure the high standards for which the Festival is famous, serving on the board from 1953 to 1971. Most of the three books about the early days of the Stratford Festival was written by Davies, with the collaboration of Tyrone Guthrie and Grant Macdonald, Boyd Neel and Tanya Moiseiwitsch.

During this period Davies was becoming known for his novels: *Tempest-Tost* (Clarke, Irwin, 1951), *Leaven of Malice* (Clarke, Irwin, 1954), and *A Mixture of Frailties* (Macmillan, 1958).

In 1961 Davies was appointed the first Master of Massey College, a new graduate college in the University of Toronto. He taught in the English Department and the Drama Centre of the University. He was also visiting professor at Trinity College. On his retirement in 1981 he was named Founding Master of Massey College.

Although Davies continued to write and publish plays, working in theatre was frustrating for him. He preferred working with publishers and editors, where chapters, incidents and choice of words were discussed politely; "you're not just told that tomorrow morning at ten we've got to have a new scene and there must be eight guaranteed laughs in it or else presumably you are going to be driven out of town like a dog." [2]

Robertson Davies' novel *The Manticore* won the Governor General's Award in 1973, and the author has received honorary degrees from twenty-one Canadian and American universities, as well as from Oxford and Trinity College, Dublin. Davies is a Companion of the Order of Canada, first Canadian member of the American Academy and Institute of Arts and Letters, Fellow of the Royal Society of Literature, Honorary Fellow, Balliol College; he has received the Toronto Arts Awards Lifetime Achievement Award, Canadian Authors Association Literary Award for Fiction, Medal of Honour for Literature from the National Arts Club in New York, the Order of Ontario, and the Canada Council Molson Prize in the Arts.

Honours and adulation continue to come to this extraordinary playwright, essayist and novelist, as Canadians and his large international readership continue to enjoy Davies' contributions to literature.

[1] Davis, J. Madison, ed. *Conversations with Robertson Davies*, Toronto: General Paperbacks, page 11.
[2] *Ibid.*, page 30.